earn your true worth

Find Greater Success in Your Professional Service Firm

David J Connell

ISBN:

ISBN-13: 978-1468144178

ISBN-10: 1468144170

Contents

DEDICATION

To my truly remarkable wife, Pat, whom I love more dearly than anyone and who has loved and supported me for so many years. And each of our children, Matthew, Daniel, Michael, Andrew & Naomi. I love each of you and as you have grown to maturity to live good lives and achieve success in your chosen careers you have made your father incredibly proud.

In the preparation of this book I thank my very good friends especially Harry Mills, author of many books of his own, for his guidance and suggestions; Steve Harris, a former Editor-in-Chief of major national newspapers, for his brilliant, experienced changes to wording and recommendations; and Andrew Mandaglio for his design work and very practical IT assistance.

EARN YOUR TRUE WORTH

Find Greater Success in Your Professional Service Firm

Chapter 1
INTRODUCTION

We are all share the same challenge, i.e. that the world is changing at a faster and faster pace...change is compounding. Experts inform us that the power of computers alone is doubling every 18 months and gaining momentum! Newspapers, magazines and TV bombard us daily with new scientific discoveries, particularly in the area of health and well-being, with announcements as to what we should now be eating and not eating. We have on the spot news 24/7. Politicians spend their days dreaming up new changes and new taxes for us and legislating for all manner of things – as if we weren't already busy enough! We have information overload and little, if any, time to think, plan & learn. Quality strategic thinking is understood as necessary for our business... but when? "Wisdom is the principal thing; therefore get wisdom: and with all your getting get understanding" (the Bible). Common sense is no longer common; in fact there are times when many of us must wonder if common sense is dead!

In the midst of all of this, professionals in accounting, financial planning, law, architecture, engineering... in all professions must somehow keep a clear sense of perspective to provide good advice to their clients. Our clients are also living in times of their greatest need and they increasingly are experiencing difficulty in securing that good advice as and when they require it. The demand has never been so great and there are many surveys highlighting this fact. Many professionals are experiencing difficulty in coping with loss of job satisfaction and all too often drastic reductions in lifestyles and quality of living. How do we adapt? What is stopping us from responding positively to these major changes in our lives? Are we winning or waning? We have so much activity that much of what many of us do is simply 'fire-fighting' – rushing around madly to put out all of those fires that keep springing up around us. With so many distractions we are less focused on our business and miss the opportunity to earn what we are worth.

The aim of this book is to provide some practical support for assisting professionals in gaining some 'life balance', success and improved earnings in their practices. I draw on over 45 years of professional consulting to many thousands of businesses including small to medium enterprises to very large corporations, and a wide range of professionals, especially accounting firms. My career began in Accountancy in 1965 through a scholarship with BHP, the largest mining company in the world. Subsequently I moved into Public Practice and became an equity partner in the largest accounting firm in Australia. Along the way I picked up specialist training, accreditation and qualifications in consulting and facilitation with a strong focus on strategic planning. Eventually after some career changes I sold my equity in a much smaller firm to my staff and established a business of practice improvement for accounting practitioners across Australia and New Zealand. This business in turn was sold to an Australian public company. This last business in particular gave me the opportunity to meet thousands of practitioners and my wife and I enjoyed a marvellous time over a 15 year period, travelling internationally, speaking at conferences and meeting and assisting practitioners on a personal basis. With over 45 years in the accounting profession, in large firms and small firms, I believe I have learned many lessons (often the hard way!) and I have been encouraged to provide a 'handbook' to fellow and aspiring professionals. Someone said that life is about trial and error, mostly error! I trust that through a reading of this book you may minimize the possible errors.

Over the years I have accumulated thousands of good books and I have developed a list of 'Must Reads' for practitioners. At the top of my list is the very popular "Man's Search for Meaning" by Viktor Frankl, described as 'Europe's leading psychiatrist'. It relates to his experiences for many years in a German concentration camp and his comments include:

- "No man can tell another what his purpose is. Each must find out for himself, and must accept the responsibility that his answer prescribes";
- "He who has a why to live can bear with almost any how."
- "In a concentration camp all the familiar goals in life are snatched away. What alone remains is "the last of human freedoms" – the ability to "choose one's attitude in a given set of circumstances."

Therein I believe lies much of the answer to our success in business and in life…understanding our purpose and choosing how we will react in any circumstance.

Definition of a Professional

When considering the meaning or purpose of our lives as professionals in particular one need only seek out the definition of a professional and I quite like the following from Wikipedia:

> "A professional is a member of a vocation founded upon specialized educational training. Because of the personal and confidential nature of many professional services and thus the necessity to place a great deal of trust in them, most professionals are held up to strict ethical and moral regulations".

Note that the earning of an income is not a primary consideration; it is an outcome of doing your work well. Most professionals I know would be horrified at the suggestion that they work for the money only. If anything the contrary is true, i.e. there is a very high level of compassion especially for clients experiencing difficulties and most will go out of the way, often at no cost to the client, to help the client through their circumstances

A Favourite Story

I recall reading many years ago the following story and it has stuck with me over the years because of its particular relevance to professionals: When a lion tamer enters a cage of wild lions he/she carries three 'tools of trade'- a whip, a pistol and a four-legged stool. Which of these is the most effective? The professional lion-tamer will tell you, to the surprise of most, that it is the stool! The whip is for show, makes a noise and to some extent keeps the lions in their place; the pistol is in a holster, not seen by the lion, and is really only there for an absolute emergency. Why the stool? These wild beasts with their large eyes see the stool being waved in front of them and their very large eyes attempt to focus in each leg of the stool at the same time. They develop blurred vision and that effectively tames them!

It doesn't need too much imagination to see the analogy for professionals. We often try to deal with too many issues at one time without real focus or prioritisation – the result is blurred vision. We can easily find ourselves 'fighting fires' as if they are of equal importance and urgency – the immediate issues in front of us – without any sort of understanding of the priorities of the 'big picture' or vision for ourselves. If you would like a good laugh go to Google and search "Monty Python - Lion Tamer". You will find an all-time classic John Cleese, 6-minute video on You Tube about a Chartered Accountant who wants to become a lion-tamer. The grass over the fence often appears greener and this interview by 'career counsellor', John Cleese, reminds us that things are not always what they seem.

Technicians

Referring back to the 'professional' definition above, our chosen vocation for a particular profession is founded upon specialised education training. In other words we are technicians in our chosen field and the majority of us love this work – we strive constantly to be better at what we do and focus strongly on improving our technical knowledge, often monitored by professional and regulatory bodies that ensure that we meet minimum standards. Clients who have invested their time and money and their trust in us are our total focus to the extent that we often drop whatever we might be doing at the time if a client should call or interrupt us. Any trust account, in financial terms, has its deposits and withdrawals and as with our services we should strive to build the 'deposits' and minimize the 'withdrawals'.

Today we have a better or improved understanding of the difference between IQ (intelligence quotient which measures intelligence) and EQ (emotional intelligence which measures the ability to assess and manage the emotions of one's self, of others and of groups). This latter measure is often described as the 'soft' skills and refers to one's leadership skills, communication skills, presentation skills, management skills, negotiation skills, and so on …our social or people skills if you like. We've all come across or heard of amazingly intelligent people who totally lack social skills. Some are just so focused on what they are good at that they exclude all else. We also know of people with good 'social' skills who couldn't lead their way out of a paper bag. Yet assuming technical and professional skill is a given it is these 'social', 'soft' or EI skills that will really determine our success in securing balance in our lives.

I quite like Ricardo Semler's ideas in his book "The Seven-Day Weekend" where he takes these ideas a step further and actually produces a formula for success he describes in his book as

IQ+EQ+SQ-EGO

Ricardo says, "For decades, IQ has created an artificial (and loaded) baseline for intelligence and capability. More recently, evaluating EQ, or the emotional content of intelligence, has become popular. Now SQ, or spiritual quotient, has been added to the equation. I mix the three together, and then subtract ego (I know I'd be in trouble with psychologists because ego includes most of the above, but I need a bit of poetic license for this home-grown theory)".

This man achieved amazing success in business and in his own life so we cannot simply brush aside his thoughts as 'doesn't apply to me' or 'a waste of time'. This is another 'Must Read' book on my list.

As I travel and meet many thousands of accountancy practitioners (in big and small firms) a common trait is this emphasis on building technical skills and keeping up to date. My business developed key performance indicators (KPI's) and has measured thousands of accounting firms. Any involvement in building or training for the EQ skills has been negligible. There is simply no formal emphasis on training for leadership, communication, negotiation, management, presentation and so on. Disturbingly, especially for accountancy practitioners who are considered to be the advisors to business managers, the management of their own business has been remarkably lacking.

This was not a result of any inability on their own part but rather the 'lion tamer' issue of dealing with the urgent, the now and what is right in front of my eyes demanding my attention. Tests have been done which show multi-tasking is less effective than doing tasks one at a time. Also multi-tasking through measures such as taking the phone call in a meeting, always leaving the phone 'on', etc. is a form of addiction: self-appreciation, self-importance, distraction, etc. To a large degree as well I have found an attitude amongst professionals, generically speaking, of " I'm an ……… (fill in accountant, solicitor, doctor, dentist, engineer, etc. as applicable)…what can you tell me? I have a degree!" Worse still there were many instances of 'management' as being beneath them… 'My time is valuable and I can't afford to waste it on trivialities!' or 'My clients need me now'.

The outcome for these people is that they become very good 'technicians' but all too often true success evades them, not just in financial terms but in family, health, social, true self-development and many other important areas of their lives. Their clients may often move on to marvellous success in their lives because of the guidance given but the professional misses out.

Who is Running the Show?

(Who is the Ringmaster of the Circus?)

As the professional practice grows the overwhelming tendency is to appoint more of the same, i.e. more 'technicians' who don't want to manage! The most common structure is that of a partnership and a 'Managing Partner' or Lead Partner is usually appointed – generally the person who has been in the firm the longest and it is his/her turn! In part that has arisen because of rules and regulations of professional bodies that require membership of the professional body to be able to practice in that particular profession. The EQ skills of management, leadership, negotiation, culture development, determining clear vision, and so on are simply not under consideration. Few, if any, of these 'Managing Partners' have had any formal training in the soft skills and they in turn fail to see the importance of this training for their young professionals and staff. Also what form of leadership is right for the organization, clients, staff, industry, and competitive forces? Is it about reshaping status quo, change, innovation, growth and so on? Get the brief right then get the right person.

The analogy of the 'lion tamer' may be taken a step further:

> • Lions are never tame. Don't assume that your people will simply follow you and act on all of your 'commands'. Remember the whip is for show.

> • Do not go into a cage without knowing what kind of day the lion is having. Most businesses now understand the vital importance of developing the right culture but many professional firms have not yet embraced these ideas and are still playing 'catch up'. Organisational culture is what people (lions) do when they are not being told what to do!

> • Lions don't learn from other lions. Professionals often explain that

'on the job' training is all that really matters. Wrong! Each individual has different and unique strengths and weaknesses. Differing personalities play a major role. Skills audits or assessments should be carried out on your business overall and tailored to your business plan. Then a skills audit is carried out for each and every person (including principals) to determine strengths and weaknesses and then tailor individual training and specific action for maximum potential.

Traditional Private Practice Model

Many public practitioners today work through partnerships. Quite a few started as sole practitioners and later merged into a partnership. Many of these partnerships have grown at a startling pace as partnerships then merge. I have considered in astonishment the growth of the firm I was involved in for almost twenty years. I worked for a time with Price Waterhouse before joining Coopers & Lybrand, then the largest firm in Australia with around $300 million in fees. Today these two firms have merged and revenue, in Australia alone today, is over $1¼ billion!

Mergers and consolidations continue at a very fast pace as smaller firms merge to get on the radar of major firms for yet further merger. The WHK Group in Australia and New Zealand seems to have come from out of nowhere and after a relatively rapid series of mergers and acquisitions is now the 5th largest firm in Australia. But there are still many thousands of smaller firms and most still operate through the partnership model. Similar examples are available in all of the professions and especially throughout America.

Who is First amongst Equals?

The partnership model has served the professions well for many years especially in that it fosters strong trust between partners who are equals. However many of these 'businesses' have grown into much larger enterprises and the question of who should lead becomes such a contentious issue that quite often no specific leader is appointed. Everyone runs the practice! Everyone has a say! And because we are technicians we have a tendency to drill down on every issue. I have encountered some quite absurd instances including the 6-partner (60 staff) firm that met weekly for six hours! No agenda or formal plan…simply met and discussed the issues (always operational). When I inquired of them "Last week what was the issue that took up most of your time?" they answered "Staff issues". I further asked "How long did this take?" Answer "Two hours". Another question: "What was the issue?" Answer: "Buying a new office chair for the receptionist!" It took ten partners and managers two hours of discussion at an average charge rate of $300 per hour…a total of $6,000 of lost opportunity to charge fees to consider an item costing about $300! As absurd as this sounds I encountered this sort of situation time and time again. Accountants being very careful professionals have all the right technical questions to ask and want to be personally satisfied that the course of action is the right one. In this instance after two hours, a decision couldn't be reached and they deferred the matter to the next meeting! In this book we will examine what really should be done at 'Partners' meetings.

As an independent observer I think that many partners meetings are like wrestling smoke or herding cats although this may be a tad hard on cats! This is management by committee and in recent times we have witnessed in my country, Australia, very extensive use of committees by Government to avoid leadership, accountability, responsibility, making decisions or as an excuse to defer a matter, perhaps indefinitely. We now have a record-breaking number of committees in this country and no real decisions being implemented. Sound familiar?

Worse still are the partners who take phone calls during partners' meetings... or even partner retreats (to consider the important strategies for the ensuing year), or take and act on messages that such-and-such a client needs attention right now! When a partner rises to leave the meeting to take the phone call, attend to the client, etc. all of the wrong messages are sent to the rest of the partnership in particular..."I really don't want to be here. Someone else can worry about this business; I have more important things to do!" It also sends out a message that this partner's organisational and time management skills are negligible. If you are disorganized and ineffective in your actions then failure will be your close companion. Also refer to my earlier comment re 'form of addiction'.

Matters are further exasperated by the role confusion of partners. Each partner is effectively wearing three (or more!) hats and when there is serious discussion it is often confusing and there is internal conflict of interest as to which role the partner is in or which hat he/she is wearing at that moment. Is it the role of the 'manager' (or technician); or perhaps the role of 'owner'/shareholder; maybe the role of 'director'? There are usually no boundaries and so we get into the discussions such as in the example above for the receptionist's chair.

Within these private practices, partners are working long hours in an attempt to sustain income levels and meet client demands. Client loyalty is a thing of the past with clients now much more willing to shop around for the best deal and they are increasingly litigious if their professional fails to deliver what they want and regulators are increasingly tough on professionals. There have been a great many large corporate court cases across the world in recent years where professionals are increasing receiving focus of attention. Clients are better informed and have many sources of information. All professions are becoming increasingly complex with ongoing changes in legislation, regulations and technology. Compliance is trumping competency and common sense to the cost of all.

The Gardener's Garden

In this environment partners become reluctant to share work with others and 'silos' develop wherein an engagement partner holds onto clients, staff and resources as much for protection as anything else. Competition arises as to who is working the hardest, who has the most staff, who has the most revenue and all too often there can be a fear that they will be forced out of the firm if they appear not to be needed. Combine this culture with the demands of clients for action now and you can begin to understand why no one has the firm's own business management as a priority for attention. The result is the gardener's garden or mechanic's car syndrome – always left to last and often totally neglected.

I recall involving a new public practitioner, who had been a Chief Financial Officer in a successful public company, in a review of KPI's for a large number of firms. He expressed total astonishment at the complete lack of attention to what I refer to as 'Cash Lock Up' i.e. the total value of the firm's funds tied up in Work-in-Progress and Debtors. It is not at all unusual to find that this sum represents six months or more of a firm's total revenue. I have seen many 'Cash Lock Up' figures usually accumulated over a great many years that equal or exceed a firm's annual revenue. The former CFO explained that because he was accountable to shareholders the external auditors would simply give him a very difficult time, to say the least, because of his inefficient controls. Who could argue with that? But then if no one in the partnership has the time or is interested who is going to willingly volunteer for the task? No one wants the responsibility. Besides at least some think that this work is beneath them.

A CEO of a major public company told me that he makes sure that sales staff does not receive bonuses until after the revenue comes in, not when the sale was made, to discourage bad practice, debt risk, etc. and improve cash flow. Some professional firms are introducing this kind of thinking but we still have a long way to go.

"I'm too busy". I've heard this so often from practitioners and I can't help but wonder if they're saying this to me are they also saying this to clients? There is a belief amongst many that "The work I do to bring in the revenue takes up all of my time and I just don't have time to focus on my practice itself". As long as you think "I am the practice", it will be virtually impossible to change. Start thinking of the practice as a separate entity and what it needs in order to grow and be successful. Consider too what you want the practice to do for you – rather than what you must do to keep the practice going. A change in thinking; a change of paradigm; a change in focus is required.

If you are thinking that all your clients want you, and that no-one can do a job as well you can, then you will be the greatest obstacle to your own practice growth.

A Coordinated Team

I was most fortunate to visit Auckland on business during an America's Cup and was able to watch the preparations and trials leading up to the main event. The activity was intense as I watched the teams move with precision and purpose and I learned something very important. These teams work amazingly well as 'teams'! Professional sailing teams invest huge sums into the design of a boat. If it can be calibrated it will be calibrated and tested over and over again to seek the smallest advantage. But I am assured that it is the human element that makes all of the difference. They try to calibrate the human involvement – language, communication, tasks and so on. So much so, I understand that most of the time the individuals are feverishly working at their particular task with total concentration – but no idea where they are actually situated in the race! For this reason a crew member at regular intervals climbs the mast to check position, wind, etc. and report back. It is the same in elite team sports everywhere. Each member knows their role for different game days, conditions, competitors, etc. and is constantly playing a slow and long game.

This checking to see where we are in the 'race' (or game), having a 'captain' (note: one only) to guide the team and issue instructions that are not confused and ascertaining what is happening in our marketplace is absolutely vital to survival let alone success. It is too easy to become inward looking and dominated by egos of particular strong personalities within the firm. In this very fast-moving world we live in market conditions can change overnight – consider fast acting computer viruses, the Global Financial Crisis, the moves to 'cloud' computing, the unanticipated 'war' for talent, and much more. Plan for the unexpected: consider whether giants like News Ltd, BP, Enron, Lehman Bros and many, many others, really did?

Even when partners are in full agreement within a boardroom as to a particular course of action to be taken these decisions can be totally undermined by a 'rogue' partner who agrees with everything in the boardroom but walks outside and does what he/she wants to do. Staff members are remarkably quick to pick up on these things and follow the example. This is surprisingly more common than realized. Planning and decision-making usually requires consensus of most, if not all, of the partners but individual partners can still block implementation. Limiting their access to information or imposing sanctions is impossible where partners also happen to own the business!

To Merge or Not?

'Economies of scale' is a frequently used term to justify decisions for mergers but a word of warning...if partners cannot agree in a partner's meeting now why would bringing in more partners change anything? My experience suggests that mergers rarely work and this has been backed up in the Australian press quoting from a high profile stock picker, John Sevior, in one of Australia's largest investment companies, taking a swipe at companies for pursuing strategic mergers and acquisitions, saying 'most of the deals were not good for shareholders'. For many though there is a window of opportunity of about 18 months to get the culture right and if it hasn't been strategically worked on prior to merger it is unlikely to happen after merger. I was involved in a corporatization of 53 independent accounting firms, all coming together formally on the one day for listing on the Stock Exchange. That's 53 different cultures (assuming they each had a tight united culture which is also unlikely!) led by something like 200 independent-minded principals – the company was fortunate to survive... for about two years.

There are of course many good reasons to merge and one is often succession. Another is in seeking an impetus for major change. Succession is a huge challenge that is far from receiving adequate attention by professional firms. An excellent American Survey produced in 2008 by the AICPA uses the word 'distressing' in their survey because of their finding that so few practitioners have faced the issue with any degree of planning or even discussion. This report is another 'must read' for the professional practitioner's library. The survey refers to many practitioners having an "eat what you kill" model of operation and at 38% of firms surveyed; "the senior partners don't feel that younger partners are ready to step up to leadership positions. One has to ask what senior partners have been doing if that many people aren't ready for leadership roles." Refer to my earlier comments on IQ, EQ and training for leadership.

Commercialization.

So what then is the solution? Well as professional firms become bigger and, yes, there is an economy of scale advantage, there is a significant move to becoming more 'commercial' in management of practices. There is an outstanding report into the accounting profession (most of which is relevant to all professions) called "The Profitable and Sustainable Practice" produced by the Institute of Chartered Accountants in the UK and Wales in January 2003. This 27 page report is full of very good information relevant to all professions and amongst other topics covers this issue of commercialization very well. It draws a distinction between what it refers to as the "Lifestyle" Practice and the "Enterprising Practice" and strongly separates the one from the other suggesting that "we have to choose the type of practice you wish to work in" - the first being one where members "view themselves as professionals following a professional vocation, and not as business people"; the second where members "make money, build capital value (for clients as well as themselves), provide a stimulating environment in which to work, embrace new technologies and which will ultimately outlive their management". I have discussed this with many hundreds of practitioners and found that most, whilst understanding the distinction, believe that there is a third type i.e. a blend of the above two and it seems to me that this is what the majority are now striving for. To my way of thinking being 'commercial' is nothing more than striving to deliver the firm's maximum potential. So how do we keep everybody happy? That is really what this book is about and in the ensuing chapters I trust that you will learn just how to tame the lions in your practice.

There are so many questions to be considered including:
- What's the desired destiny?
- Is it sustainable, viable, valuable?
- Are there other options?
- Who shapes this?
- Who will make it succeed/fail?
- What assumptions have been made?
- Have they been tested?

Waste

Waste is a fact of life in all businesses and professional firms. Toyota, as part of their ongoing efforts to become more efficient identified seven wastes and their waste audit process has been adopted worldwide (a Google on 'Toyota's seven wastes' produced 134,000 hits!). I have adapted the process to accounting firms and identified waste or 'lost opportunity' cost in many firms with astonishing outcomes. There is now no doubt in my mind that every professional firm has at least 20% waste. When this is converted to revenue $'s for lost opportunity the sum involved is always material in total. For example if we assume a firm with $1 million fees and productivity of say 50% after write-offs (not at all uncommon in professional firms!), then 20% represents $400,000 – all potentially could have gone straight to the bottom line but instead to the waste bin!

From my experience much of this comes from a lack of focus on standard business procedures and policies and more often than not an accumulation of a lot of small inefficiencies. Principals in their drive to keep costs down are often unwilling to outlay money or staff resources on the latest software (or even hardware) training and implementation and yet are most anxious to take their regular 'drawing' of cash for private purposes. This is false economy and any business that is not prepared to invest in the development and growth of the business will never achieve its full potential. To my amazement many firms cannot see the value of setting aside time and resources for the waste audit process and instead question the cost of the exercise! The value to be achieved depends upon the size of the firm but in the above example we are addressing value at around 10-20 times the cost (refer in a later chapter to Managers v. Leaders).

I am firmly convinced that most professional firms have a very long way to go in achieving efficiency in the conduct of their business management. It is almost as though we are the last bastion of resistance to change in our business management. Quite frankly, when I am engaged to assist firms in their business management I find that I am usually starting from a very low base. Improvements are not that difficult to find. In the case of accounting firms we are talking about the professionals in business management. Accountants are dealing on a daily basis with their clients' business improvement and it is quite an anomaly to find that their own businesses are generally not managed to their real potential and worth. Greater accountability is required with proper processes so that greater priority is upon management of the firm's $'s as opposed to management of the client's $'s. Who has responsibility for getting up every morning and focusing on efficiency?

Don't confuse efficiency and effectiveness…we need both.

Imagine if clients could see behind closed doors! Again this book seeks to address this anomaly for all professionals in practice.

CHAPTER SUMMARY

- Change is compounding. We have information overload and little, if any, time to think, plan & learn.
- The aim of this book is to provide some practical support for assisting professionals in gaining 'life balance'.
- Victor Frankl – "No man can tell another what his purpose is. Each must find out for himself, and must accept the responsibility that his answer prescribes."
- Earning of an income is not a primary consideration for most professionals; it is an outcome of doing your work well.
- The Lion-tamer story – trying to deal with too many issues results in blurred vision.
- We are technicians in our chosen field and most of us love this work.
- A formula for success – IQ+EQ+SQ-EGO.
- Who is running the show? Get the brief right then get the right per-son. Who is first amongst equals.
- Traditional private practice model – partners meetings are like wrestling smoke or herding cats! Typically we have management by committee.
- The gardener's garden – always left to last and often totally neglected. "I'm too busy". "I am the practice".
- Focus is required.
- A coordinated team with precision and purpose. Calibrate and test over and over again.
- To merge or not? If partners cannot agree in a partners' meeting now why would bringing in more partners change anything? There is a window of opportunity to get the culture right and if it hasn't been strategically worked on prior to the meeting it is unlikely to happen after the merger.
- There are of course many good reasons to merge and one is often succession.
- A distinction between "Lifestyle" practice and "Enterprising" practice. We have to choose.
- Waste – every professional firm has at least 20% waste. When this is converted to revenue $'s for lost opportunity the sum involved is always material in total

CHAPTER 2
BUSTING THE MYTHS:
THE PROFESSIONAL
ILLUSION OF PROFIT

10 of the Dumbest Things You can do in your Firm

A gardener's garden is often the least maintained garden; the mechanic's car often sits waiting for attention; a solicitor's Will is often missed; and perhaps it should come as no surprise to us that accountancy firms are often not the most efficient and effective professional firms managed. Why is it that this anomaly applies across the full spectrum of professional firms?

Perhaps we are simply too busy looking after our client's affairs to focus on our own business; or maybe we are hoping that someone else in the practice has their eye on the ball!
Sure we attend practice meetings and we analyse and argue and ensure that costs don't get out of hand. We query debtors, WIP, productivity, workflow......... and then we leave the boardroom to go back to looking after clients!

Practice management is non-chargeable—we can't waste time on these matters can we? Someone less skilled or talented should do that shouldn't they? And yet my experience shows that most practices have a great deal of waste and because we are not practicing what we preach we miss out on the opportunity for better profit and a more efficient firm. When a firm seriously focuses in their own management substantial improvement in results usually follows. I have seen firms improve their net profit by up to five times through simply paying more attention to their own practice.

We are trained professionals, specialist advisors and one would expect that we would also know how to manage. So why do we do dumb things in the management of our own firms?

The following are ten of the dumbest things you can do with your firm:

1.   Don't bother to do any strategic planning. This takes time and money and we have to produce dollars today. Tomorrow will take care of itself. Beside there is so much work to do why do we need to have a strategic plan? In any event we want to allow flexibility for everyone to do what they want—after all we're professionals and professional flexibility is important. These 'vision' and 'mission' people are in cloud cuckoo land! We've been around for a long time and we'll survive whatever comes our way.

2.   Take on any work that comes in the door. So long as they have the smell of a cheque book on them, we'll take them on even if no one else will. Don't worry about any sort of screening and culling, we need the work don't we! Worry about pricing later—if the fee's too high we'll just take a write-off. Besides we can always employ more people—just keep them busy! We've heard of the 80/20 rule and the 140/20 rule (140% of net profit comes from 20% of customers) but we're different—we are professionals; and the standard business management rules don't apply to us.

3.   Ignore Debtors & WIP lockup. A few months in debtors and WIP are OK—it all comes in eventually. Besides the bank will always fund us a bit more if we need it. It's all cash in the long run. Why waste money employing a person to manage and monitor this—we don't want to upset the clients. Many of them are having a tough time and they don't need aggravation from us!

4.   Assume timesheets, costing records and our financial statements are always right and a good indicator of value. Timesheets are a costing system aren't they? Always accurate, we rely on them for fees determination. Don't worry about write-offs; if we have to take them we don't like it but that's life. Never write-on—that's just not the done thing. If the client gets outstanding value from us then that's his/her good fortune. We've decided upon our rate per hour and there's no changing that decision once it's made. Don't bother about recording 'support' time directly relating to clients such as phone calls, filing, secretarial, fees preparation, secretarial and so on. These are all 'admin' and can't be charged.

5.   Never use an 'outsider' as facilitator, mentor or coach. We are trained, experienced professionals—what can they tell us? Besides there's a cost involved and regardless of any value received, it's still a cost that we can do without.

6.   Ensure all partners/principals have an equal say in every decision—including all operational activities such as, for example, acquiring an office chair for the receptionist. Such an important decision requires the input of everyone even though our individual time might be worth $300 / hour plus! What does it matter that the 'lost opportunity' time in making these decisions might come to more than the item under discussion! We know that delegation to a practice manager or administration person would make sense but we need to know individually what is going on don't we?

7.   Delegation doesn't work in our practice. Sure there are some things that I can delegate but in the main no one else can complete the important tasks as well as I do—besides mistakes will be made otherwise and I'll only have to re-do the work anyway. In any event I just can't find the right staff.

8.   Use computers and software for as long as we can without

updating. That way we save a lot of money and keep our costs down! Don't worry about the rapid changes in IT— we'll wait and see what happens and eventually we'll catch up.

9.   Training—we haven't got the time or money for any serious training besides we are flat out just keeping up with legislative changes. We don't have time for any soft skills training such as leadership, public speaking, report writing, communication skills and so on. Professionals don't need this! We had enough of this at Uni!

10.   Networks—join a network and find out what other firms are doing—what! And waste more time away from the practice. What can they tell us that we don't already know?

Now I suspect that at least some of these have may have brought a smile to your face but believe me, I have witnessed all of these...and all too frequently. These are just some of the dumbest in my perception. There are many more. Can you name some?

Complacency Breeds Complacency

When it comes to profit many firms are complacent. So long as the bills are being paid and I draw a reasonable sum each month why should I worry? That raises a most interesting question...just how much is enough? I frequently ask principals/partners in workshops to write down on a piece of paper just what they think their profit should be? Invariably there is a very diverse range of opinion and there should at least be some attempt by partners to come to agreement on a suitable amount. But the point I wish to make is that a large sum is inevitably left on the table. Complacency breeds complacency and as long as partners are reasonably satisfied a serious effort to change is unlikely. Yet most professional firms invest so little in areas like innovation, staff training, the latest technology, professional marketing, systems and procedures improvement, furniture and equipment, office presentation, and much more. If there is cash in the bank at the end of the month then a suitable drawing is on the cards! So few firms complete a budgeting exercise that drives the firm. Ideally the overall firm budget for the year/s ahead should have a number of budgets branching off and supporting it where a serious drilling down is evident. I refer to the Personnel Budget, the Work-in-Progress and Debtors Budgets, the Capital Expenditure Budget that itemizes future investment in equipment especially information technology, the Training Budget that links into the skills audits and individualizes or tailors the training needs, the Marketing Budget, the Cash Flow Budget as distinct from the 'accruals' Profit and Loss Budget, the Balance Sheet Budget, the Drawings Budget, and all of these should link in so that 'what if' scenarios may be considered up front. The DuPont analysis is also an outstanding tool for assisting in these projections.

Now I did say 'ideally' and the reality is that this sort of detailed and drilling down enables decisions to be made in advance and not on the run. For example, what percentage of our revenue should we outlay on training? What is realistic to enable us to grow our people and skills to reach the vision we have already determined in our Business Plan and strategies? In light of our growth projection what is a reasonable percentage to spend on marketing in order to achieve that growth. This should lead to what I refer to as 'laser beam' focused marketing rather than the scattergun marketing that most professionals engage in (if any marketing at all!).

I came across a firm that argued strongly that accruals or management accounting was unnecessary in their practice. "We record everything on a cash basis and it is much the same as our tax recording". Now, unfortunately I have to tell you that this was a very fast growing accounting firm and they really were quite innovative and had credibility and respect in one of our network groups so that when they spoke out on this issue others did tend to listen. However they made a major decision to move from time sheet billing to value billing within the same year. They carried this out remarkably well with the result that they were able to pull in up to three year's revenue (last year's outstanding's, this year's revenue and next year's agreed fixed price) in cash in one year. Naturally their reports showed an outstanding year BUT…the next year…the cash dropped dramatically because they had already effectively received payment in advance for much of their work and they found themselves in a real bind. My understanding is that the practice has now virtually disbanded.

It really goes without saying that short cuts in professional firms, when it comes to reporting on a true management basis, must be avoided. Most professional firms work on the 'rule of thumb' if 1/3rd, 1/3rd, 1/3rd, i.e. 1/3rd of revenue is taken up in overhead, 1/3rd of revenue is absorbed in wage costs and 1/3rd remains for profit – suggesting that professional firms should earn 33⅓ % 'net' profit but this is where the 'illusion' of profit comes in. Because no adjustment is made for realistic 'commercial' salaries for principals, or interest on capital and current accounts this simple formula can lead to complacency. And note that the interest is calculated at commercial rates and after regular, realistic revaluation of Balance Sheet items – especially Goodwill, Intellectual Property and other intangibles. In a later chapter I explain in greater detail the options for calculating commercial salary.

Where these adjustments are made in a commercial manner invariably I have found that 'Net Profit' (before tax) drops dramatically to around 5% pa or less. Losses are not uncommon. In my experience listed corporations on the stock exchange generally seek a return in the order of 15-20% pa or more – and they are punished in their share prices if they don't, so accountability is very strong. It seems to me that this is a reasonable minimal guide for professional firms. Return on investment should also be examined (allowing for revaluation of the intangibles). Is the firm receiving a reasonable return on their investment after the above adjustments?

So where is the net profit we should be earning? Waste is a big factor and time sheet recording for many professionals has made us lazy. There is a strong move to value pricing, i.e., a more serious examination of the value to the client and negotiation and management of expectations with the client. I am not advocating cessation of the time sheet system; I am simply advocating a return to the use of time sheets as a costing system that is a reference point only (as originally intended), not the means of calculating the bill. As already explained when professional firms have such low productivity there is something seriously amiss.

You simply must take the management of your professional practice at least as seriously as you do when attending to the needs of your largest client. This book will provide you with an approach to truly earning what you are worth but you must be willing to take action, apply resources and make decisions. The practice cannot run itself! And avoid being misled by the illusion of strong profit.

CHAPTER SUMMARY

- Why do we do dumb things in the management of our own firms?
- A list of ten of the dumbest things you can do with your firm.
- Complacency breeds complacency. As long as partners are reasonably satisfied a serious effort to change is unlikely.
- Short cuts in professional firms, when it comes to reporting on a true management basis, must be avoided.
- The 'Rule of Thumb' that provides an illusion of profit – the 'three times' rule.
- Take the management of your professional practice at least as seriously as you do when attending to the needs of your largest client.

CHAPTER 3
THE CHOICE IS YOURS!

Let us return just for a moment to Victor Frankl's quote in the Introduction and in particular this part:

"What alone remains is "the last of human freedoms" – the ability to "choose one's attitude in a given set of circumstances""

Our freedom and ability to choose always remains with us as individuals – so why don't we choose to make the decisions we know that we should especially when it comes to such an important matter as the efficient management of our own practice/business? In the introduction we have touched upon some of the antics and actions that partners get up to when it comes to decision making and leadership but we need to dig deeper into our human consciousness to find some answers.

D x V x P = Formula for Change

Some of the answer may be found in a formula (professional's love formulae). The official 'Formula for Change' was created by Richard Beckhard and David Gleicher (pioneers in the field of organizational development), around 1969, and is sometimes called Gleicher's Formula. And it suggests that three factors must be present for meaningful organizational change to take place. These factors are:

D = Dissatisfaction with how things are now;

V = Vision of what is possible;

F = First, concrete steps that can be taken towards the vision.

If the product of these three factors is greater than

R = Resistance,

Then change is possible.

This formula has been dusted off and improved over the years and more recently I have seen it described as the DVP formula where F is changed to P = Plan. If we apply scaling to this formula we can actually obtain a percentage result.

When dealing with a new client, mentally I will often run this formula through my head and also ask my client to make their own assessment (note: this is not intended to be a pedantic exercise but rather a feeling as to 'what it is like around here'). I suggest a scaling of 1-10 for each factor and so we can consider the following example –

D x V x P = Propensity for Change (or Resistance)

10 x 10 x 10 = 1000 (maximum score)

Dissatisfaction

So for the first factor, i.e. Dissatisfaction, the opposite end of the scale is total complacency. My experience in working with accounting firms and other professionals is that complacency in the management of their practices is very high indeed. Dissatisfaction is usually not a high score. Quite the contrary. On a first visit inevitably I hear statements like "You'll like what you see here…we are an amazing firm with great culture, great people and great systems" i.e., all is good in our garden!

By the time I arrive I have usually done some homework and in one instance where a similar statement was made to me on the drive from the airport to the office, I replied, "That is really good news but tell me, in my calculations I have found that your average practice (total) recovery rate is only $45/hour (see later for details as to this calculation) – if that is in fact correct something is seriously wrong in your practice". Initially the partner strongly disagreed that this could even be possible but as we worked through the calculation he came to realize that I was right and turned quite pale. As we arrived at the boardroom, even before he had introduced me to his three partners, he was explaining to them with great concern this KPI that I had raised. The level of dissatisfaction in that practice suddenly went through the roof – 10 out of 10 – and we were off to a good start with propensity for change.

The term "Status quo" (of our firm) is often used by practitioners, probably without an understanding of its full meaning. It is Latin for "not yet optimal" – always room for improvement and if not, then going backwards. Arguing to preserve the status quo is usually done in the context of opposing change. To argue to maintain the status quo means that we are accepting the fact that we are not yet 'optimal'! Dissatisfaction can often be declared but we need to dig to find the more fundamental, unanticipated, unspoken 'elephants in the room'.

When I commence a new assignment I seek out quickly the hot buttons that get the blood pressure up and if I get a strong reaction of dissatisfaction I read that as a strong positive, good sign. On the other hand if I am unable to lift the partners out of their complacency I have to decide whether in fact this firm has any propensity for change and if I come to the conclusion that the answer is "No" then the best decision I can make for all is to walk away because nothing I do is going to change anything. I have been known to reject an assignment – much to the consternation of the firm involved. You can lead a horse to water, but you can't make it drink. You can give people all the information in the world, but you can't make them think!

Vision

So if we have agreed that change is necessary, what do we want to change to? What is our Vision of the firm at some time in the future? Questions such as:

- What is our purpose?
- What profit do we want?
- What profile?
- Competitive in what areas?
- Customer satisfaction?
- What quality?
- Staff retention?
- Succession?
- What do you want the firm to look like when it has fully developed or matured?
- How will it look and feel?
- How will you know it's working?
- How will clients know it's working?

....are just some of the questions to be answered.

Inevitably little, if any thought has been given to this and if there are a number of partners the vision can be quite confused. Professionals are busy people and will say that they don't have time for 'daydreaming about the future'. True, time is of the essence and whereas large corporations and organizations have resources, money and time to allocate 'project teams' to work through issues that can take months practitioners simply do not have that luxury. I found over the years that any time I required from partners simply had to be productive to the maximum and eventually I developed a three-day workshop: two days with the partners and one day with staff. This may be reduced for a sole practitioner but for two or more partners it is the absolute minimum and requires full attention (no phone calls or interruptions). I was also able to streamline a lot of the activity, for example, rather than start a SWOT

(Strengths, Weaknesses, Opportunities & Threats) I started with a templated example and changed it as appropriate.

Ideally, time permitting, individual interviews with partners will assist greatly in determining what they consider to be the vision for their firm. Inevitably there will be much variation between partners. However, achieving this is rare. Most of the time it is considered to be a major achievement if we can secure ALL partners in a workshop for two days without interruption! So the process becomes vital and securing a good, experienced chairman/ facilitator even more so (more about this later). One of the early questions I ask is, "How much do you wish to earn?" the amount will vary from partner to partner but at least some broad idea as to net profit emerges. Most professionals will be aware of the basic rule of thumb known as the "Three Times Rule" which basically states that in any examination of a Profit & Loss of a professional firm, one-third of revenue is outlaid on salaries, one-third on other overheads and one-third is left for profit. If we accept this and we know the profit we want then simply by multiplying this profit by three times we can determine our desired revenue. From there we can focus on the necessary strategies to bridge the gap between the revenue figure now and the revenue figure we desire to achieve our net profit. Note that this is a very generic rule-of-thumb and many firms today strive for a higher multiple of salaries in order to achieve a better net outcome.

However, there is much, much more to Vision than earning a desired income. My approach has been to seek to paint a clear picture of what the practice actually looks like three or five years out. An attempt is made to think about a picture of your practice that you could draw if necessary with all the detail clearly mapped out. My starting point here is another generic rule-of-thumb known as the 'Rule of 72'. Financial professionals will recognize this as the rule of thumb for calculating compound interest. Put simply, if you invest $10,000 in the bank at 10% per annum, compounding, your investment will double to $20,000 in 7.2 years. The answer is found by dividing 72 by the interest rate, i.e. 72/10 = 7.2. Apply this to the growth of your firm. If we know from say the last three years that your firm is consistently growing at the rate of 10% per annum, net, then revenue will double in 7.2 years. Accordingly, if your firm is currently generating $1 mil in fees then in 7.2 years it should be around $2 mil in fees. This has a lot of implications and begins to raise questions to assist you in clarifying your 'picture' or 'vision':

- Will the staff numbers double also?
- What recruitment procedures and policies do we have in place to secure the additional staff?
- What is our culture – are we seen to be an employer of 'first choice'?
- Do we have adequate training in place?
- Do we have adequate processes and procedures?
- Is our software up to date and able to meet the requirements of this growth?
- Is our hardware up to date and able to meet the requirements of this growth?
- Do we have adequate space to accommodate our people?
- What specific strategies are required to ensure this growth continues?
- Do we have a marketing plan?

...and so on – this not intended to be a comprehensive listing but starts to raise the right sort of questions and the right sort of conversation. Over the years I have developed a series of questionnaires for this exercise.

Plan

This third and final factor is about the sort of planning we currently have in the practice. Based on many years of experience my assessment would be that most professional firms have little or no planning of value. It is not unusual to discover firms that at least have an annual review or 'retreat' to consider how they are progressing but more often than not these are simply 'talk fests' with little or no organization or process. In the very large firms the likelihood is that any planning is attended to by consultants with very little input from the people who matter – the partners and staff. Often someone ticks a few boxes and hands this over to the consultant!

I recall receiving a phone call from the managing partner of a 6-partner firm. He was quite disillusioned. He explained that every year for many years his firm arranged a retreat (or 'advance' as he called it!) at a luxury resort over three days. Despite this the firm seemed to be making little or no progress in improving management. I inquired whether they had kept any notes of the last meeting and would it be possible to send them to me. Upon receiving them I reviewed them carefully and noted the following:

> • An agenda had not been prepared to provide some structure to the three days.
>
> • The notes indicated that discussion was all over the place with no real control or direction.
>
> • Using a yellow highlighter I identified 46 issues in the notes.
>
> • Of these 46 issues only one was 'strategic', the rest were operational, i.e. day to day management issues such as staff matters, productivity, debtors collection, billing, etc.
>
> • There was no attempt to list the issues they had themselves identified.

41

- There was no prioritisation of issues.
- There were no specific action plans or decisions made.
- Need I say more?

It was agreed that a new Strategic Planning workshop was required and I was engaged to facilitate a three-day intensive exercise. On the first day as we commenced, the body language and conversation was quite obvious – most of these people had an attitude of "Here we go again – what a waste of time?" However we worked to the set process and it emerged that their major issue was growth! They were growing at the quite remarkable rate of 30% per annum. Use the rule of 72 above and it becomes apparent that they were doubling every 2.4 years! They had no adequate recruitment processes and were not keeping up with the required staff numbers. There were no budget projections – no one had the time to do this work. Everyone was under enormous pressure and this was a highly stressed organization. Securing the staff numbers required on an ongoing basis was seen to be impossible and they began to think through the process of deliberately reducing growth. It was agreed to cut the growth rate in half to 15% per annum and strategies were determined to support this. Today this practice is very much under control and now has a clear vision for direction.

I recall another assignment where I was specifically instructed to 'just facilitate'…no processes and little input from me. Two large 'second tier' firms were merging and two full days (true!) had been set aside to 'negotiate' values. I carried out the task as requested and this meant that everyone had to be given the opportunity for a say (about 40-50 partners in the room). The room was full of prima donna, egotistical people who had very strong ideas about the values they wanted in this 'new' merged firm. I was astonished at the final listing…many pages in length…totally overdone with 'blurred' values but surprisingly they were very pleased with their own efforts. I just could not see this working out – there were no action plans to ensure implementation, just simply a list. My concerns were enhanced when I became involved, during a tea break, with two junior/new partners from opposite sides of the merge firms. They didn't mind my presence at all and were discussing whether to stay in the profession or not because they each had young families and were finding the pressures of work was impacting very seriously upon their life balance. The discussion convinced me that what was being discussed as values in the meeting room simply did not exist in their real world.

Through other discussions I formed the opinion that these two merging firms had very different values and cultures. The outcome was that within a few short years the two firms demerged.

Let us now revisit this Formula for Change:
D x V x P = Propensity for Change (or Resistance)
10 x 10 x 10 = 1000 (maximum score)

Now enter your own scores for your firm:

… x …. x …. = …….. Convert this to a percentage if you wish.

The lower your score the less propensity your organization has for change; the higher the score the greater the propensity for change. A good leader needs to build a case for change by explaining in detail the shortcomings of the existing system and commence by building the current level of dissatisfaction.

Fear of Failure

There has been much written about the ability to "choose one's

43

attitude in a given set of circumstances" but the fact remains that in the professional world there are so many who exhibit this reluctance to change and the question remains, "Why don't we choose …and make decisions for a better life, better business and so on". Psychiatrists, Psychologists and others far more capable than I have written whole text books on the subject but in the context of professionals running their lives and businesses it has been of particular interest to me.

Fear of failure is one of the reasons. We build up in our minds barriers… the pain, the time, the money. Often there is an attitude of "We've tried this before (without really trying too much) and it didn't work". There can be a fear of retribution if we get this wrong. Most of the time though these barriers are only in our minds and when we seriously take on these barriers and confront them we get through. Some readers may have come across the acronym often used – FEAR: False Expectations Appearing Real. It does seem to be a human trait or failing that we tend to imagine things to be worse than they really are. If we are 100% risk averse, then we will do nothing and in every firm there will be partners who are highly risk averse. 'Doing' builds knowledge and capacity…even through error.

Locus of Control

Psychologists have also developed a term to describe the extent to which individuals believe that they can control events that affect them. They refer to it as Locus of Control and Wikipedia provides us with the following very good definition:

"Understanding of the concept was developed by Julian B. Rotter in 1954, and has since become an important aspect of personality studies.

Individuals with a high internal locus of control believe that events result primarily from their own behaviour and actions. Those with a low internal locus of control believe that powerful others, fate, or chance primarily determine events.

Those with a high internal locus of control have better control of their behaviour, tend to exhibit more political behaviours, and are more likely to attempt to influence other people than those with a low external locus of control. Those with a high internal locus of control are more likely to assume that their efforts will be successful. They are more active in seeking information and knowledge concerning their situation.

One's "locus" (Latin for "place" or "location") can either be internal (meaning the person believes that they control their life) or external (meaning they believe that their environment, some higher power, or other people control their decisions and their life)".

Pareto's 80/20 Rule

Now allow me to introduce yet another Rule of Thumb, this time the very well-known 80/20 rule or Pareto principle. Pareto observed in 1906 that 80% of the land in Italy was owned by 20% of the population; he developed the principle by observing that 20% of the pea pods in his garden contained 80% of the peas. Today we have learned the rule applies to a whole range of issues – a popular one in professional firms being that 80% of our revenue comes from 20% of our clients (I have confirmed this time and time again). I have experimented with this rule of thumb and it is really quite surprising just how consistent it is. For example, consider the clothes hanging in your wardrobe…you wear 20% of the clothes 80% of the time. With this in mind I culled old suits and clothes that I rarely wore and donated them to charity. This gave me much more room but had minimal impact on the clothes I wear on a day to day basis. In the above context it is also my view now, from experience, that 80% of our partners, staff and clients have an 'external' Locus of Control whilst only 20% have an 'internal' locus of control. 80% of a firm's drive, profit and culture also comes from 20% of our people. In other words 80% of our people, in particular think that events are outside their control. It is wrong thinking but it is real and goes some of the way to explaining why decisions are not made. These people require strong leadership and direction and need convincing of the reasons for change through, for example, the D x V x P formula above. Lift their level of disappointment to realise that 'things have to change around here' and can change; improve their vision as to what is possible and the clear benefits to them as individuals; put in place action plans so that everyone is aware of the specific steps we have to take.

One senior, very successful executive explained to me -

"I have always had a rule of thumb that five people matter more at every level and are the 'keys':

e.g. only five Directors on any Board,

e.g. only five senior executives,

e.g. only five of their key reports each, and so on"

Sacred Cows

Another book on the 'must read' list ... 'Sacred Cows Make the Best Burgers' (Robert Hriegel and David Brandt). The book refers to two definitions of 'Sacred Cow': one, a cow considered as holy in origin and immune from normal treatment – allowed to roam freely often causing destruction and chaos; the second, an outmoded belief, assumption, practice policy and so on that inhibits change and prevents responsiveness. 'Sacred Cows' do roam freely in our professional practices and to an independent observer the chaos is often unbelievable. The book sets out what is described as "Paradigm-busting strategies" and makes for excellent reading. Many of your people are comfortable and complacent with the way they work and they 'fear' change. Quite often too, previous attempts at change have fallen flat and their battle cry is "It hasn't worked before why will this time be any different?" The challenge for a good leader is to awaken the imagination in these people to just what is possible.

Always ask "why do you/we do it this way?" 80% of the time the answer will be "Because we have always done it this way!"; "Just the way it is"; or "That's what the policy says."

Involve Your People

If we begin to bring together our thoughts above on D x V x P, Locus of Control and 'Sacred Cows' then you can begin to understand and perhaps wonder "How do we actually get anything done around here?" When I commence a strategic planning assignment I begin with two days of intensive workshop, using a process, with the partners/principals, then a full day with staff and I always emphasize the importance of the day with staff. The first two days are about intensive brainstorming to determine just what is it that these owners of the business want to achieve and can achieve but then staff has to be involved to take ownership of these ideas and to awaken their imagination as to possibilities. Inevitably I have found that once the ideas are placed in front of your people and their opinions sought there will always be new and often very significant issues raised by staff that partners had not considered. Never underestimate the ability of your people to rise to the occasion when seriously given the opportunity. Despite this I have still encountered firms that leave staff out of the equation because of either a cost saving measure or the belief that their people have nothing to contribute! When this happens the likelihood of success is reduced dramatically. If you underestimate staff, they will underestimate you!

Elephants Can't Jump

Don't think for a minute that big firms with access to greater resources are immune from any of this or that they are capable of resolving matters more efficiently. The reality is that the larger the firm the bigger the issues and the more challenging the barriers that can often be more deeply embedded and camouflaged by headline "success", profit and so on. Again, think Lehman Bros and other GFC (Global Financial Crisis) victims. Another good book for your list ... 'The Elephant and the Flea' (Charles Handy)...or as he also describes it 'Looking Backwards to the Future'. Having worked with the largest mining company in the world (BHP) and the largest accounting firm in Australia at that time (Coopers & Lybrand) out of sheer frustration I often used the expression 'Elephants can't jump (and of course they leave a great mess behind them!)!' Quick decisions when required just are not possible because of the processes, procedures and protocols – in other words, red tape that triumphs over purpose, people and profit!. Either you adjust and accept the situation you are in or you get out and the author of this book explores the future where he believes the 'fleas', that is the small independent operators, will take over from the huge elephants of old. All the signs I see at present indicate quite the opposite – mergers, acquisitions and consolidations in our professions move forward unabated – but, as one of those 'fleas' now I like what I read in this book and we are seeing many large organizations now establishing small groups or teams within their large structures and these teams being given full authority and accountability for action.

Use a Facilitator

Why do we need a facilitator or person often referred to as a 'coach'?

What is the "secret" behind successful people ... Lee Iacocca, Bill Gates, Eleanor Roosevelt, Paul Newman, Vince Lombardi, Oprah Winfrey, Michael Jordan and Tiger Woods?

The secret is ... they all had a coach or mentor to guide them and to bring out the best in them!

What's the "difference" between them and you? .....Perhaps you haven't had a coach or facilitator yet.

What Facilitators Do

• Facilitators help their clients to think, talk and target better goals and then help them reach those goals.

• Facilitators ask their clients to do more than they would have done on their own.

• Facilitators focus their clients better to produce results more quickly.

• Facilitators provide their clients with the tools, support and structure to accomplish more than they think possible.

• A Facilitator can help you identify that incremental change that makes all of the difference to your firm and your success.

• Facilitators can ask the awkward and sensitive questions.

Successful sports people have discovered these lessons a long time ago, e.g. the national NZ Rugby Union team - the "All Blacks", Michael Phelps (16 Olympic medals), the Australian Netball team, Mark Webber, Cadel Evans and so many others. I mentioned in the Introduction the America's Cup and when they design a winning boat, if anything can be calibrated it will be calibrated and tested over and over again to seek the smallest advantage. But I am assured that it is the human element that makes all of the difference. They try to calibrate the human involvement – language, communication, tasks and so on.

To achieve this 'calibration' of your firm you require an experienced, skilled facilitator/coach. This person should have specialist training and know how to draw out issues and discussions from your people. A 'consultant' is the wrong sort of person. A 'consultant's' task is to give specific advice on specific issues – tells you what to do (as one CEO friend of mine says… "a consultant comes in, takes your watch, and then charges you to get the time!"); a facilitator or coach helps a group work together to reach the best possible conclusions or decisions themselves. The facilitator encourages full participation. I have come across some most unusual appointments such as the accounting firm that appointed their local church minister and another accounting firm that appointed a local insurance agent. One would have to assume that these people possess skills not immediately obvious for the task at hand! Unfortunately many 'facilitator's' or chairpersons I have come across have had no formal training, qualifications or experience in the role and it can become a case of the blind leading the blind or the blind leading the bland!

A further risk is to use one of 'your own', usually a partner. In order to achieve successful outcomes the facilitator should be a skilled professional with a thorough knowledge of strategic planning processes and how to draw out the best in your people. A partner will usually not have the experience of working with many organizations in this field and invariably lacks the big picture as to what is happening in the wider marketplace of the profession. There is also the strong possibility that, not being independent, a partner will have his/her own barrows to push, or will "chair" and not participate as an equal, and ego and ambition are likely to interfere. I have seen too many prima donnas running professional firms. Personalities play a strong role and whereas a professional facilitator would seek to draw out discussion from the more reserved, conservative people and attempt to achieve balanced discussion, a partner is unlikely to achieve the outcomes desired. In my experience many professionals do not understand the difference between 'operational' and 'strategic' issues and like the lions tend to focus on what is right in front of them, inevitably the operational, day-to-day issues, with the resultant blurred vision as we saw previously in the example of the six partners holding an annual retreat in a luxury resort – these meetings simply become talk fests. It is also my observation that professional groups tend to have more than their fair share of egomaniacs that tend to dominate conversations.

Mission

Just a brief note on 'mission'. 'Mission' is not 'Vision' and these are often confused. If we turn to Wikipedia we can obtain some good clarification:

> Vision: Defines the desired or intended future state of an organization or enterprise in terms of its fundamental objective and/or strategic direction.

> Vision is a long term view, sometimes describing how the organization would like the world in which it operates to be. For example a charity working with the poor might have a vision statement which read
> "A world without poverty".
> Perhaps in simple terms: "What do we want?"

To my way of thinking Vision is quite simply a picture, one we can draw if requested, of our business at a time in the future…a snapshot of what we want our practice to look like.

Again we turn to Wikipedia for an explanation of Mission:

> Mission: Defines the fundamental purpose of an organization or an enterprise, succinctly describing why it exists and what it does to

51

achieve its Vision. A mission statement provides details of what is done and answers the question: "What do we do?" For example, the charity might provide "job training for the homeless and unemployed"

Again, in simple terms as stated above: "What do we do?" The 'mission' relates back to my comments at the outset in this book under the heading 'In Search of Meaning and Purpose' and in the same way as we need to determine our own private purpose in life we should attempt to do the same for our practice. This is serious, high value, work and requires much effort and thought – it is, in my opinion, not something that is arrived at in an afternoon workshop. Unfortunately there is much nonsense and wasted time that takes place in this matter. I recall when I was working in the (then) largest accounting firm in Australia, a Mission statement was proclaimed. Staff and partners across the country were advised of a major announcement and at the same time we were herded into our various darkened boardrooms to watch a video which was the grand proclamation by the then chairman of the firm. The following was to be our new mission, in gold coloring, mounted in a gold frame, hung in the reception of every office:

(Name deleted) is an organization of outstanding people committed to meeting our clients' business needs by providing excellent advice and the highest standard of service, with independence and integrity. We maintain this position by fostering respect for the individual and encouraging personal development, initiative and innovation through teamwork. We sustain the highest levels of technical knowledge and skill by investing in people and programs, fulfilling our commitment to provide the highest quality service and advice. By adhering to this philosophy we are rewarded by personal and professional growth while being part of a world-wide team of professionals.

As I best recall there was a lot of sniggering and even laughter as everyone left the room. No one, as far as I am aware, amongst the partners or staff had any input whatsoever into its preparation, therefore it could not possibly be a 'mission' for the firm …one agreed upon and reflecting the values of all of its stakeholders. A consultant had been paid a lot of money to prepare this well-worded document but inevitably it just became some words in a picture frame on the wall for promotional purposes. That, I am afraid is what happens with most 'mission statements'. My own experience was that these words did not permeate the organization; the culture did not support them; and the leaders did not 'walk the talk'.

On the other hand this is the McDonalds mission statement:

> "McDonald's vision is to be the world's best quick service restaurant experience. Being the best means providing outstanding quality, service, cleanliness, and value, so that we make every customer in every restaurant smile."

> The confusion between vision and mission is apparent in McDonald's mission statement but nevertheless it is simple, to the point and I suspect that most of us probably agree that 'Yes, this is McDonald's purpose!"

A Due Diligence on Your Own Firm

When I began my experience in the planning process the idea of building a 'Business Plan' was a relatively new concept and only the very large enterprises could afford the resources to do so. In the large accounting firm I was working with I was able to secure not one but three manuals of that firm's processes for preparing business plans – one from London, one from Sydney and the third from Melbourne! They were all very comprehensive and very different. The use of questionnaires was very popular. The final business plan was usually a very thick document and I often wondered whether the firm charged by weight rather than by value or hours!

The reality at the time was that these comprehensive business plans contained far too much information and were often not fully read and absorbed. Their complexity created confusion. Information is not insight. Formulae are not foresight. Today simplicity is the key and any plan in this fast moving world we live in must be dynamic, i.e. allows for variable or constantly changing nature. The overall process can be broken down into three simple steps:

> **NOW :** what does our firm look like right now; compare with other similar firms; conduct a due-diligence on our own firm; identify all deficiencies and shortfalls; review financial position. The definition of competition has also been turned upside down. Every business can now be in someone else's business and global. For example banks are now looking more closely at providing legal and accounting services!
>
> **VISION :** where are we going? Do we have a very clear picture with all features identified for what we want in say three years or five years? The best client service may no longer be in a rival professional firm. You may have to look to McDonald's, FedEx, Toyota and similar successful organizations to see how they operate. There is a good saying: "I have seen the enemy and he is us"
>
> **IMPLEMENTATION :** the vital step. What are our main strategies and objectives? What specific action will we take? How will we monitor our ongoing performance?

Before you gather together in a workshop to consider your firm's future direction it is important to carry out a comprehensive analysis of your firm's current position. There is what I consider to be a most amazing book called 'The Consultant's Tool Kit' edited by Mel Silberman. This book provides free downloads including 45 questionnaires…take your pick!

Ideally, compare your key performance indicators (KPI's) with other practices in your profession. Many organizations now provide extensive comparison information for relatively low price. Some of the more important ones in my view are:

- Net profit
- Average Net profit per partner.
- ROI – return on investment (include value of Goodwill and any other intangibles).
- Average Gross Revenue (billings) per partner.
- Average Practice Recovery Rate – see note below.
- Productivity percentage.
- Net Profit per client.
- Debtors days.
- Work in Progress days.
- Cash lock up days (total of the last two).
- Revenue per staff member (all personnel).
- Direct Wages & salaries as a percentage of revenue.
- Deficiencies and write-offs as a percentage of revenue.
- Staff Training direct cost as a percentage of revenue.
- Total Number of Clients
- Brand Recognition
- Brand Value
- Average Revenue per client
- The 80/20 Rule analysis of clients

- Source of Fees by Service
- Staff per Principal
- Net profit per Principal per Hour

I consider the Average Practice Recovery Rate to be a very strong indicator of performance. It is in my view a key driver and it is a relatively simple calculation as follows:

Calculate the total available hours in your practice by multiplying the full-time equivalent (allows for part-time personnel) number of personnel (everyone – staff, partners, support) by 1680 hours per annum. This figure may vary a little from State to State, country to country, but it is the standard that I have used for many years. The answer is the total number of available hours you have after annual leave and public holiday (assuming 9-5, 5 days per week). Then divide the total available hours into your total annual revenue and the answer is the average revenue that you have earned per hour across the total firm. The result may shock you and it is a calculation I use often to shake firms out of their complacency. Partners may well be charging good rates per hour for their output but this often overlooks all of the personnel supporting the partner and their lower rates or non-recovery can drastically bring down a firm's total recovery. The "headline" is not the story!

Although the above list may appear to be a long list it is not a fully comprehensive one. These are all financially related and the non financial KPI's are often more important. For example 'job turnaround time', the culture of your firm, training programs, systems development, marketing programs and so on.

Strengths, Weaknesses, Opportunities and Threats (SWOT)

This need not be too elaborate an exercise and I use the following simple template:

STRENGTHS	WEAKNESSES
OPPORTUNITIES	THREATS

The following is an actual example of a completed template for an accounting firm:

As a starting point you may wish to move through these lists deleting, changing and adding as appropriate for your practice. I have found that commencing with a template such as this can be very time saving. Because SWOT concentrates on the issues that potentially have the most impact, the SWOT analysis is useful when a very limited amount of time is available to address a complex strategic situation.

STRENGTHS	WEAKNESSES
• Team works well together : good culture • A great team environment • Commitment • A strong propensity for change : not afraid of change. • Good leadership : led by example • Personalities of principals • Encouraging a learning environment • Innovative • Reputation • Respect is high • High values : integrity, honesty • Strong work ethic • An established, long-term client base : captured market • Trusted relationship with clients • Good service • Cost of services kept to a minimum. • Personal selling – our personalities. • Statutory need for accounts • Base of recurring fees • Client inertia - it's difficult to move to another accountant • Independence/objectivity/integrity as ethical base • Experience of many businesses at different levels • Depth of knowledge • Consultancy based on detailed knowledge of clients' transactions • Intellectual quality 'chartered' enhances the brand • Ability to deliver the 'hand holding' service - quasi finance director for small companies • Measurement skills • Youth and energy of firm. • The drive and enthusiasm and passion to do better and to add value to clients. • Turnaround for output • Location , exposure : been here for 80 years ; established • Financial planning now established : working with other professionals	• Lack of differentiation in the market and in the product • No unique selling point (USP) • Often perceived as knowing the cost of everything and the value of nothing • I didn't know you did that' - poor marketing skills • Don't break down the service to devise a system • Developing people skills – soft skills • Giving away advice • Chargeable time as basis for billing culture • Poor communication within firm, poor sharing of knowledge leads to slow learning • Principals 'too busy' • Don't analyse what they do for clients • Uncomfortable with selling • Don't really understand the business they're in • No written marketing plan • No Business Plan at this time • Confidence • FTI – failure to implement and follow through. • Work flow monitoring. • Client expectation of access to Principal • Industry staff shortage – crisis. • Job turnaround • Low productivity • Low practice recovery rate

OPPORTUNITIES	THREATS
• Good core client base • Small business consultancy • Tax planning services (better pack-aged) • Assurance services • Key product is business planning and Strategy • Regulation brings opportunities • Technology • Competition don't market them-selves well • The starting point is so low, any-thing would be an improvement! • Alliances with other consultants • Target 'niche' clients e.g. Restaurants & CFO roles – outsourcing. • Client categorization • Packaging of services • Expanding regional branches	• Image of accountants – staid, boring! • Competition from other disciplines - sales, IT, law, MBAs. Business Coaches • Ability of unregulated competition to take business • Less barriers to entry in non-regulated areas • Technology • Can't deliver tax, audit and consultancy the same way • Difficulty in attracting good people • Succession • Lack of ability to exploit the marketplace • Consolidators • Dropping student numbers reduces mid-tier management availability • Leaking knowledge/information • Partners Health or accident. • Damage to reputation – 'credibility'

The following diagram shows how a SWOT analysis fits into a strategic situation analysis.

Situation Analysis

/ \

Internal Analysis External Analysis

/ \ / \

Strengths Weaknesses Opportunities Threats

|

SWOT Profile

The internal and external situation analysis can produce a large volume of information, much of which may not be highly relevant. The SWOT analysis can serve as a filter to reduce the information to a manageable quantity of key issues. The SWOT analysis classifies the internal aspects of the company as strengths or weaknesses and the external situational factors as opportunities or threats.

Strengths can serve as a basis for building a competitive advantage, and weaknesses may hinder it. By understanding these four aspects of its situation, a firm can better leverage its strengths, correct its weaknesses, capitalize on opportunities, and deter potentially destructive threats.

Internal Analysis

The internal analysis is a comprehensive evaluation of the internal environment's potential strengths and weaknesses. Factors should be evaluated across the organization in areas such as:

- Firm culture
- Firm image
- Organisational structure
- Key staff
- Access to resources
- Position on the experience curve
- Operational efficiency
- Operational capacity
- Brand awareness
- Market share
- Financial resources
- Exclusive contracts
- Patents and trade secrets

The SWOT analysis summarizes the internal factors of the firm as a list of strengths and weaknesses.

External Analysis

An opportunity is the chance to introduce a new product or service that can generate improved returns. Opportunities can arise when changes occur in the external environment. Many of these changes can be perceived as threats to the market position of existing products and may necessitate a change in product specifications or the development of new products in order for the firm to remain competitive.

Changes in the external environment may be related to:

- Clients
- Competitors
- Market trends
- Suppliers
- Partners
- Social changes
- New technology
- Economic environment
- Political and regulatory environment
- Public engagement (media, lobby groups, special interests, social media)

The SWOT analysis summarizes the external environmental factors as a list of opportunities and threats.

SWOT Profile

When the analysis has been completed, a SWOT profile can be generated and used as the basis of goal setting, strategy formulation, and implementation.

A Google search on this subject produced almost 3 million hits so there is very widespread use of this process and much explanation and information available as to its use. It would be surprising if you are not already aware of this process and some would brush this aside as 'been there; done that'. The reason for showing all of this information here again is to refresh your thinking and to encourage you to take a simple approach through the above template. My recommendation is that firms should carry out a SWOT every six months.

Strategic SWOT

Once you have completed this SWOT exercise which in itself is a very valuable exercise I encourage you to take the next step which is referred to as a Strategic SWOT. The SWOT analysis is generally seen as determining where a business is now, however the Strategic SWOT analysis can provide a framework for the review of strategy as well as for the development of strategy. It is one methodology only but one I have found highly useful in stimulating thinking. It is one of my favourite consulting tools. The process involves matching the internal environment with the external environment and asking the appropriate questions. The following is an actual case for a 6 partner firm:

1. How can I use these strengths to commercialize these opportunities?

2. How can I use these strengths to overcome these threats?

3. What do I do to make sure that these weaknesses don't spoil these opportunities?

4. What if the weaknesses combine with the threats? What corrective action will I need to take?

As you can see we arrived at 20 specific strategies when we focused upon just the top 3 or 4 items from each category. This is too many strategies to deal with (refer the Lion Tamer story in the introduction) and so from these what three or four strategies will have the biggest impact on your organization? This firm chose these:

	Strengths	Weaknesses
	Established long term client base	Productivity & Recovery rate
	Reputation & Relationships	Giving away advice
	Good Service	FTI (failure to implement)
	Financial Planning	Too busy
OPPORTUNITIES	How can I use these strengths to commercialize these opportunities?	What do I do to make sure that these weaknesses don't spoil these opportunities?
Diversity in range of services	1. Develop new value added services	7. Standardize processes
Building a great team culture	2. Develop a management accounting team	8. Implement an intranet system
Expanding regional branches	3. Acquire new businesses	9. Build courage to bill the client – recognise value
Categorise clients	4. Clearly identify "A" clients and prepare one page plans for each client	10. Delegate more/ team building
	5. Build on the 'client manager' concept.	11. Develop a marketing plan
	6. Build soft skills through the whole practice	12. Complete a full budget that drives the firm
	7. Systematize referrals	
THREATS	How can I use these strengths to overcome these threats?	What if the weaknesses combine with the threats? What corrective action will I need to take?
Technology	13. Focus on our top clients – one page plans, etc.	17. Improved delegation of tasks
Loss of a partner/ Succession	14. Improved , focused , skills-audit based training	18. Consider establishing a tax shop
Retention of good people	15. Systematize / McDonlaldise your practice	19. Appoint a leader in management accounting – a champion of the cause Leaking knowledge
	16. Better staff incentive programs	20. Publicise targets

1. Complete a full budget that drives the firm

2. Clearly identify "A" clients and prepare one page plans

3. Delegate more/ team building

Issues

By now your firm should be developing a comprehensive list of issues requiring attention and do not forget to involve your staff – more often than not they will identify issues that partners will not. And don't forget the lion-tamer still needs someone to feed the lions, wash them and clean up the cages! I had one case where we set aside a day with approximately 30 staff and when I asked the question "what issues do you think the firm needs to address?" it almost seemed as if there was no stopping them. They identified 75 issues! Through a process of voting and elimination these came down to about six issues when it was realized that virtually all issues related to communication within the firm. 'Internal communications' was not an issue on the partners' list!

By now complacency about your firm should well-and-truly have dissipated. I have yet to come across a firm that doesn't have at least 30 issues requiring attention. Anything less suggests to me that they haven't taken the exercise seriously enough.

It is important to get every issue identified and onto your list and join the dots to identify core/common/connected issues and opportunities. This is where a good facilitator proves beneficial. In professional firms it is not unusual for partners to get involved in what I refer to as 'conversational ping pong' – the light issues; not the 'heavy' ones! It is not at all uncommon to overhear a conversation at the commencement of the week: "How was your weekend? Are the kids well? Who won the football?" …and more, without any real interest in the answer. Respect and trust do tend to be very strong in most firms between partners but the 'real' issues; the 'heavy stuff' is often left alone so as not to rock the boat. It is the facilitator's task to dig deep and draw out these issues to be placed on the table no matter how difficult they might be to talk about. I have come across firms where partners simply do not talk to each other at all and in one case, at a meeting I was engaged to facilitate, a cup of hot coffee was thrown at another partner amidst much loud yelling and colourful language…the instant coffee was an instant revelation! That firm did separate – with my assistance!

Sometimes it is necessary to slam the heavy bowling balls onto the table and bring whatever is simmering underneath to the surface. Not a pleasant task but people working together will follow human behaviour: "get along" to "get along", which means blinkers, earplugs and silence on core pressure points. The day-to-day working under the same roof can be highly stressful to the point of impacting upon a partner's health if not resolved. Staff members are not blind either and often find themselves in a position of having to take sides whether they wish to or not. Culture of the firm deteriorates. Client services, if partners are not working well together, are affected as well.

I recall a case that I have referred to as 'Shades of Underbelly' ("Underbelly" is a popular TV series about real gangland wars, crooked police and crime in Australia). This 3 partner firm had been operating for over twenty years despite the fact that at least two of the partners had very deep dislike, to put it mildly, for each other. People don't have to like each other. Many organisations have succeeded despite some deep personal animus between team members. But it wasn't allowed to impact professional preparation, planning and performance. When this firm engaged me all was positive and I had no idea of the deep simmering of discontent or the fact that they had previously engaged at least three professional mediators and had ignored their advice. Within a month of my involvement accusations of fraud, lies, a death threat and much more emerged. One partner suffered depression. It was quite a shock to me. To the outside world these were very highly respected professionals and advisors but inside it was a complete cauldron of simmering, bottled up feelings. The term "velvet coffin" has come into use in our language today and it is often used to describe a loveless marriage to a wealthy man or a prison for the well-connected. It could be used in our context here to describe those who become so comfortable in their job, earnings, status, routine and so on that they don't realise they are dying! To cut a long story short I was able to convince these partners to separate and split the practice and to the best of my knowledge they are now each happily in control of their own destiny.

It's interesting how irrational professional people can become when a formerly close relationship has broken down altogether. Perhaps what happens here is just simply a reflection of what happens in our wider society. Divorce lawyers are very familiar with this. Levels of intelligence seem to make no difference to the degrees of irrationality. I have many more examples of stressed firms and I could write a book just on these. It still amazes me though that people are so willing to continue in these stressed situations or perhaps more truthfully seem unable to make decisions or understand that …the choice is yours!

CHAPTER SUMMARY

- Our freedom and ability to choose always remains with us as individuals – so why don't we choose?
- Some of the answer may be found in the formula for change – D x V x P or Dissatisfaction x Vision x Planning.
- Dissatisfaction – opposite to complacency. There's always room for improvement. Look for the unspoken 'elephants in the room'.
- Vision – What do we want to change to? Paint a clear picture of what the practice actually looks like three or five years out.
- Plan – Many firms hold annual 'talk fests' without any real process or focus. Most firms have little or no planning of value.
- Fear of Failure – we build up in our minds barriers…the pain, the time, the money. Most of the time though these barriers are only in our minds.
- Locus of Control – a distinction between internal and external belief as to our ability to control events in our lives.
- Pareto's 80/20 Rule – the rule applies to a whole range of issues the attitude of our clients, partners and staff.
- Sacred Cows – they roam freely in our professional practices and to an independent observer the chaos is often unbelievable
- Involve Your People – staff must be involved to take ownership of ideas and to awaken their imagination as to possibilities.
- Elephants can't Jump – The larger the firm the bigger the issues and the more challenging the barriers that can often be more deeply embedded.
- Use a Facilitator. The "secret" behind many successful people is that they have a coach or mentor to guide them and to bring out the best in them.
- What Facilitators Do – facilitators help their clients to think, talk and target better goals and then help them to reach those goals.
- Mission – the fundamental purpose of an organization. What do we do? The confusion between vision and mission clarified.
- A Due Diligence on Your Own Firm – three simple steps: Now, Vision, Implementation.
- Strengths, Weaknesses , Opportunities and Threats (SWOT) – a template, example and explanation.
- Strategic SWOT – this provides a framework for the review of strategy as well as for the development of strategies.
- Issues – what issues do you think the firm needs to address…a comprehensive list. It is important to get every issue identified.
- The choice is yours!

CHAPTER 4
A MASTERPLAN

Changes in the marketplace are compounding at an alarming rate in speed and complexity and one would imagine that external pressures on firms cause the most failures. Most failures however are related to internal problems. Any firm failures are mostly attributed to a failure of management including a lack of skills, poor resource management, no strategy, no forward planning, continuous firefighting of issues, being internally focused and not responding to changes in client's needs. Many professionals are also risk adverse, hold on to outdated processes, convince themselves that fee cutting will retain their client base, and are reluctant to let go of ownership and control.

As a firm grows many of the approaches, processes and systems adopted when they were small will not work as they get larger. Unfortunately many simply muddle along hoping that somehow things will get better!

I have often pointed out that the Rule of 72 applies to a partner's work-load. So if a partner keeps taking on more and more work he/she eventually becomes totally overcommitted. This happens much quicker than many realize. The reluctance to delegate can have a most serious impact. If for example a partner takes on just 10% extra workload per annum then that workload doubles in 7.2 years! 20% extra workload doubles in 3.6 years. Work isn't completed on time, fees are unrendered and clients complain about poor quality service. Cash flow and relationships then become a major problem! Sound familiar?

Develop Strong Focus

In this day and age where we are experiencing a war for talent – skilled, experienced people are becoming harder and harder to find as birth rates decline around the world and economies continue to grow (albeit in some countries at a slower rate) – matching resources to our workload becomes a greater challenge. In these circumstances we cannot afford to be complacent or accept waste at the levels of the past. Global accessibility has improved; movement of people is more efficient and there is declining loyalty. We have no choice but to be more focused. The trap is, as I have pointed out at the introduction, being focused on too many issues and trying to address all at once – the blurred vision! Perhaps we require some sort of special bifocals that enable us to see the long view (strategy, vision, etc.) and to see the immediate, pressing issues? One of the challenges to us is that if we walk with our head always up and focused on the horizon we will not see the pothole; if we walk with our head down all the time, we will not see the pole!

If you have already completed the due diligence on your own firm by now you could quite easily have 50 – 100 issues! Hopefully the dissatisfaction rating has lifted strongly, the vision is beginning to become clarified and a plan is starting to emerge (remember D x V x P).

Hard decisions are required. A stronger focus on clients is required. It is no longer possible to take on every assignment that comes through the door. Culling and screening becomes necessary. We need to challenge our assumptions (sacred cows!) that every client should be looked after personally by a partner. We may have to accept that there are some clients we are better off without! Again the 80/20 rule tells us that 20% of our clients produce 80% of our revenue. Time and time again, despite protestations from my clients this rule has proved correct. There is also another less known rule called the 140/20 rule. Once again this is a broad rule of thumb but once you understand its implications it makes a great deal of sense. It suggests that 140% of your NET profit comes from 20% of your clients. I love the look on the faces of accountants as they try to come to grips with this with some often suggesting that this is impossible. However let's examine this a bit closer:

20% of clients produce 140% of net profit

Therefore, 80% of clients produce (40%) of negative net profit

– or net loss

Now, without being too pedantic or focusing on the accuracy of the 140/20 split the message is clearly that you can make a large increase in your Net Profit by simply upgrading or removing clients that produce a net loss or low contribution to profit. My experience has taught me that most professionals do not calculate net profit or loss per client. Instead there is usually a sigh of relief if there is no write-off or deficiency. This calculation usually requires some assumptions in relation to overhead and salary allocation but it can be done and is worthwhile.

Tough decisions are required here – perhaps this is really a once off loss on this client because of extraordinary circumstances? In such a case it may be well worth absorbing the loss for the future benefit…be sure though that there is a future benefit. I would encourage firms to establish a limit above which the Board (Partners' Meeting) must be involved in decision-making for any approvals. I have often encountered situations where individual partners in their earnest desire to look after the interest of their client overlook the best interest of the firm and we have a serious conflict of interest. Unfortunately I have seen too many examples where a net loss is taken year after year after year without any real examination as to why we should continue to do this as a firm. If a partner has a strong personal reason maybe that partner should carry the loss?

I have also come across a sole practitioner who had over the years accumulated over 40 honorary audits and had received little or no acknowledgement for his generous support. Supporting your community for deserving causes is a marvellous commitment that every firm should make but be aware of the extent of your commitment. Many of these audits had seen change of personnel and there was an expectation of the accountant to fulfill this duty with much pressure often being applied. My recommendation to him was 'start culling immediately' and where honorary audits are retained, calculate the fee and arrange an exchange of cheques so that the donation is clearly recognized in income as a donation or gift. I further recommended that consideration be given to charging cost price, i.e. usually around 2/3rds of what would be a normal fee (refer back to the three times rule of thumb).

A Masterplan

Your overall focus should be under six major areas –

- **SERVICES** to your clients
- **PROCESSES** and procedures, standardised through your firm
- **ORGANISATION** and structure of your firm
- **LEADERSHIP** one overall leader only but everyone supporting that leader when key moments arise and strong support is warranted.
- **COMMITMENT** by your people

…and underlying and integral to each of these is

- **PEOPLE**

The Service that you provide is the focal point for the rest. Quality of service is impossible without quality in the processes and procedures. Quality in processes and procedures is impossible without the right organization or structure. The right organization is meaningless without strong leadership. Strong commitment is the support base for all the rest and your people are what makes all of this happen.

These provide the foundation upon which you can build a truly amazing firm.

Many firms are organized around individual partners and have grown like Topsy (from Uncle Tom's Cabin: ***"I s'pect I just growed. Don't think nobody never made me."*** says Topsy, a wild and uncivilized slave girl). Over time these separate groups become like silos with each partner heading his/her own silo. Work pours in through the top of the silo and comes out the bottom – perhaps to a support group, and then to the client. Within each silo it is likely that you will find staff loyal to their respective silo leader and vice versa. It is further likely that they will have developed their own way of doing things ignoring any attempts to develop a firm approach to processing work. I have witnessed a discussion in a 6 partner firm where a partner argued for a large increase in salary for his 'manager'. It became quite heated with the partner prepared to fight strongly for his 'manager'. The problem, however, was that the other five partners had no idea whether she, the 'manager, was worth the extra increase or not and they in turn felt the competitive need to argue in support of their own managers!

I have also seen a 9 partner firm with nine of these silos! Effectively this was nine sole practitioners sharing the rent. The 'managing partner' ruled with an iron fist…it turned out his family interests owned the building and his conflict of interest mean't that this firm was unlikely to ever move to a greater co-operative team. You could cut the air with a knife – the suspicion between silos of principals and staff was quite obvious. There was an incredible sense of competition between the groups – even to the extent of competing for clients. When I walked into their reception I was almost bowled over by the number of staff keen to help me…until I mentioned that I had an appointment! The culture of this firm could only be a negative one fraught with simmering feelings and competitive views. The partner who had called me in was very aware of the firm's problems but a meeting with the managing partner made it clear that change was unlikely and I walked away. My advice to the partner who invited me was to do the same.

Some firms may thrive on 'creative tension' or divisional competition but this is only sustainable over the long term if there are clear rules, rewards, discipline and accountability.

The lack of focus by many firms for strategic planning and direction is appalling. I couldn't believe my own ears when a smaller 2 partner accounting firm, in a small country town, advised me that they thought planning was a waste of time. They were happy to just go with the flow…a luxury some professions and firms can afford…in good times and for a short time!. Complacency was at a very high level and they were convinced that their performance as a business was second to none. No real score in 'D x V x P'. Shortly after my visit a major business in their community closed its doors and I understand that this has had an impact on the entire community. In the normal course of events one would expect this will also impact upon the firm. In the same community a strong competitor moved into their immediate neighbourhood. It will be interesting to observe how this firm copes with change in these fast moving times we live in.

CHAPTER SUMMARY

- Develop Strong Focus – we cannot afford to be complacent or accept waste at the levels of the past. The trap though is being focused to many issues and trying to address all at once – the blurred vision!
- Hard decisions are required. We need to challenge our assumptions (sacred cows!).
- A Masterplan – six major areas:
  - Services to your clients
  - Processes and procedures
  - Organisation and structure
  - Leadership
  - Commitment
  - People
- The lack of focus by many firms for strategic planning and direction is appalling.

CHAPTER 5
LIFE BALANCE

Before we move on to address these six major areas …a word or two about something we all pay much lip service to. This is such a common topic of interest at so many business meetings, conferences, dinner parties, BBQ's and other social gatherings that one would assume that most professionals have great 'life balance'. Unfortunately the opposite is all too common.

There are definitely exceptional cases and for a profession that is just sometimes labelled 'boring' I know of many accounting practitioners who live remarkably exciting lives. Let me give you a few examples of people I personally know-

- A chartered Accountant with a major firm who represented Australia in Rugby Union.
- A CPA who represents Australia in polo.
- A former grand prix super bike racer who continues his super bike racing as a hobby and regularly loads up his huge van with bikes and supplies and takes his family and staff to races.
- The tax specialist, who has parachuted out of planes, raced super bikes and in particular she has abseiled down the Hilton Hotel Building in Sydney.
- The sole practitioner who regularly takes his staff deep sea fishing.
- The walking enthusiast who enters many of the larger walkathons and similar events and has walked across Australia's Simpson Desert.
- The practitioner who drove on old car 3000k's across Australia in a huge motoring fundraiser.

- The two-partner country firm where both partners play Rugby League and Rugby Union most weekends during the football season and their staff and families are their main fans. Based in a country town in western Queensland they travel around four hours to a game!
- The partners and staff who surf regularly together at their local beach before going to work.
- Numerous practitioners who do outstanding work on an honorary basis in their communities.

….just to name a few!

But these are the exceptions.

There has been so much written on this subject that one would assume that everyone knows how to balance their lives. A Google on 'life balance' has produced 88 million hits! Many best seller books have covered the subject. Authors such as Stephen Covey, Michael Gerber, Brian Tracy, Dr. Phil McGraw and Jack Collis are just a handful of names of authors I have read. All have value. The most commonly used tool for coaches is the 'Wheel of Life' and the internet provides a quite remarkable treasure trove of variations of this tool. Many if not most large corporations have provided training in this important area dating back many, many years. Could anyone realistically not have come across this concept at some stage during their lives? So everyone has their life in balance, right? Wrong. So very few have. Is it worth the effort to try? Of course it is but the road to hell is paved with good intentions… good intentions without actions will lead you nowhere but down. I'm sure that we all have a good intention of winning the lottery one day too but the odds are stacked against you and you have to buy an awful lot of tickets to have just a minimal chance.

Personal Experience

Perhaps it's best if I share my personal experience here. I was not an avid reader of books. Then in February 1994 I was given a book by a very good friend and mentor. His name is Brian Kahlefeldt. He has achieved amazing success in his life and I took the view that if he is giving me a book to read then, without doubt I should read it. This book was a turning point in my life and within a month I had met with the author in his home. We remain friends to this day. The book is "Yes You Can" written by Jack Collis and as he points out in his book, "The longest journey starts with the first step". I decided, I chose, to take that first step and began to set goals in the manner outlined in his book. One of those first steps is to consider just what are the most important areas of your life? Since then I have facilitated many 'life balance' workshops, mostly with accountants but also with doctors, and I ask the question what do you think are the most important areas of your life? In one workshop we came up with a list of twelve areas and invariably the first area to be mentioned is not work related and about creating wealth but rather 'family'. This raises an interesting observation: most of us clearly recognize that our family, our loved ones, is our top priority in life yet where do we give most of our time and resources…. work related matters. I am reliably advised by experts that this is the major cause of underlying stress and tension in our lives. We know what we want to and should do but for a variety of reasons take a different direction.

Most Important Areas of Your Life

Over the years I have narrowed this list of twelve important areas, determined by attendees at my workshops, down to six main, all inclusive areas shown in this chart:-

Life Balance

If you search on Google you will find a variety of examples – the above are the areas of importance as determined in our workshops. I have established specific goals in each of these areas for myself and over the years they have changed, as my family has grown for example. In the area of 'Family' I had developed some unfortunate habits without realizing it. My wife, Pat, had tried to explain to me that our five children were growing up quickly and I could be missing out on many of the good parts of their lives because of the extensive time I spent on work related matters. My career was very absorbing of my time and I did find it very challenging to change my ways. My written goals in each of these areas where very specific with clear steps, for example in the section labelled 'family' I created sub-headings for my wife and each of the children, then under each name listed the goals I had for improved time with each of them. One of the items under my wife's name was to take her to at least one musical every year. We live 500 k's from each of Sydney and Melbourne so this involved an overnight stay and dinner. 15-16 years later we have attended over 45 musicals in Melbourne, Sydney, Brisbane and London. Additional time with each of our children involved attending their sporting activities, school events, assisting with homework and later university degrees and so on. Weekends, especially Sundays became fully fledged family days. Today our children are in their late twenties and early thirties and they talk frequently of the good times when they were growing up. We are a remarkably close family even though distance now separates us. Apart from the usual holiday, birthday and anniversary gatherings we also hold a special 'Connell Muster' weekend where we do something special such as climbing to the very top of the Sydney Harbour Bridge, a luncheon cruise on Sydney Harbour, dinners, lunches, football, winery tours etc. With the benefit of hindsight I am convinced that if I hadn't made those specific goals and implemented action (and continue to do so) life would be very, very different for me today.

A Confession

Now at this point I'm going to make a confession. Over the years I have met many thousands of professionals but not come across one who has taken the steps that I have above. Most if not all have agreed with my actions even though often I receive a look of disbelief but they have not taken the action. Perhaps this says a lot about me. Perhaps it says a lot about professionals. I don't know but I do know that my life improved dramatically as a result of the action I took. These steps led me to selling my accounting practice to my staff and taking up a career of support in practice improvement for professionals, speaking engagements across Australia and New Zealand, the extensive travel that this involved, making amazing friends across the two countries, writing this book and much, much more.

Take Control of your Life

I am firmly convinced that if you don't take control of your life, someone else will…and to their benefit, not yours. You have the freedom to choose your path in life but so many, the majority, do not ….perhaps anticipating that someone else will make decisions for them! They will and it will be all about pursuing their path…their purpose in life. Never get so caught up in the detail of getting your work done to satisfy clients, keeping staff happy and productive and coping with all the day-to-day demands of a practice that you do not have time to focus on the bigger picture and the more important priorities of your life.

The game of life requires that you learn the necessary skills quickly. Unfortunately nobody has ever really taught you the rules and whether you like it or not you will create your own experience and there is a time clock. You have 168 hours per week, no more, no less. What you do with those hours is vital. Do not lull yourself into complacency or a false sense of security of, as we often hear in Australia "It'll be alright mate!" You do choose the behavior (the action), you do choose the consequences. Life rewards action, but not action for the sake of action. It must be action focused on the important.

Dr. Victor Frankl made his choices in the face of unending atrocities. The SS guards could not control what attitude he took about his sufferings. They could not force upon him how he would interpret and react to his treatment. You can, in any situation, choose your reaction and your life must be actively managed …by you! Many friends and business associates of mine where in shock when I recently took a year off. But they were also surprised when I pointed out that it represents only 2% of my expected life span, i.e. one year out of 80. The fact is that I have enjoyed a marvellous rest, special time with my wife, written this book and enjoyed some special holidays but also had much time to just think and I am now resuming a professional career with a revamped approach and very excited and enthusiastic about my future plans. We do need to reinvent ourselves from time to time.

CHAPTER SUMMARY

- Could anyone realistically not have come across this concept at some stage in their lives? So everyone has their life in balance, right? Wrong. So very few have. Is it worth the effort to try? Of course it is but the road to hell is paved with good intentions.

- Personal experience …a gift book from a friend book – "Yes You Can" written by Jack Collis.

- The most important areas of your life – family, health, career and wealth, philosophy, social and fun, and growth and self-development.

- A confession – most , if not all agreed with my actions even though I often receive a look of disbelief but they have not taken the action.

- Take control of your life – if you don't, someone else will…and to their benefit, not yours. You have the freedom to choose.

CHAPTER 6
SERVICES TO YOUR CLIENTS

(Ring the Bell for Service)

The services we offer our clients, whatever profession you belong to, is the focal point for purpose and achievement. This becomes the rallying point for quality and productivity. Once again, refer back to Viktor Frankl and his 'search for meaning and purpose'…"He who has a why to live can bear with almost any how." Our individual answer goes a long way to explaining why we are in our particular profession.

There is much research now to support Victor Frankl's view that concentration camp survivors who had a strong belief in life and had a why to live survived longer and better than those who did not. "Belief" in professional sport is a key driver of success, because talent is common and is a given. Games are often said to be won "between the ears", not between the goal posts!

Doctors for example are usually people of truly great compassion and purpose to assist people to better health. Accountants I suggest also have compassion with a purpose to assist people to better wealth. I suspect that if you continue to carry out a similar examination of every profession you will find a calling or vocation to make a difference to people's lives. You will find plenty of examples of professional 'technicians' who may give the opposite impression but that doesn't mean that they are not driven by a clear purpose to help people. A specialist doctor may be the absolute pinnacle of his/her profession but have a dreadful 'bedside' manner, for example the popular British TV series, "Doc Martin". That doesn't mean that he/she isn't very serious about the service – he/she is so technically involved in working through the highly complex issues in finding the right solution that it is not always easy to explain the process in simple layman's terms.

There is an added challenge for dedicated professionals to motivate employees and the larger the firm the more difficult this challenge. There is often very different attitude and motivation involved. One of my favourite stories on this subject is the following:

> Three labourers were busily swinging sledgehammers in a large excavation for a new city building. When the first was asked "What are you doing?" he answered, "I'm breaking rocks." (…and probably thought to himself, "What a stupid question – surely it is obvious to anyone with eyes?"). When the second was asked, "What are you doing?" he responded with more enthusiasm, "I have the task of ensuring that this particular corner of the site is cleaned up thoroughly in readiness for a concrete pour." When the third person was asked, "What are you doing?" he responded very enthusiastically, "I'm part of this marvellous project to build a cathedral."

Everyone is building something in the way of a product or service and it almost always involves shared effort with others to form a combined final service (or product). It is important therefore that each participating employee or professional feels ownership and accountability for their particular contribution. Once again, quoting from Viktor Frankl "No man can tell another what his purpose is. Each must find out for himself, and must accept the responsibility that his answer prescribes". From this it becomes obvious that if we are telling our people day in and day out what to do without assisting them to understand the big picture or vision how can they be enthusiastic and committed? We need to be certain about the direction we are taking and very clear about the business we are in.

A common purpose is essential for success but few professionals are good at identifying it and explaining it – very few have a mission and goals that employees can relate to and 'own'. This might be clear in the mind of an individual practitioner (saving lives, building wealth, healthy teeth, etc.). Most employees have a need to feel pride in their work and the practice they work for. Good leaders understand this and pay attention to strategically building and reinforcing an appropriate culture. All too often though this is poorly managed and staff are held responsible when things go wrong. If I had a dollar for every time I have heard the statement "Why can't we get good staff these days?" I would be a very wealthy man. In many practices the divide between principals or partners and staff has become highly polarized. I have actually been part of a major firm where your level or position in the firm determined which floor of the building you worked in …starting with partners on the top floor. Turnover of staff at this firm was over 30% per annum…one guess why! Small firms are not exempt and, again, I have witnessed, more than once, the kind of management that can only be described as a dictator …or perhaps more kindly an autocrat. The Golden Rule of "Do unto others as you would have them do unto you" applies just as much, if not more, in professional practices as it does in life generally. Manager others as you would like to be managed.

Quality in the service follows from the collective team effort – and that flows from pride and professionalism. Pride is the motivation or fuel of human accomplishment. Pride and quality go together. If you are not making the effort to instill pride in your workers the quality of your service will suffer and it is quite apparent just how obvious this can become when one simply observes the behaviour of the 'director of first impressions', i.e. your receptionist. Over a period of many years I made it a habit to chat to the receptionist (all too often I was kept waiting in any event!) and the first question I would ask is "Do you know and understand your firm's mission?" In the majority of cases the blank look said it all (they may well have been thinking … "this guy is a nutcase!"). Another question was: "Do you enjoy working here?" You would be amazed just how honest many people can be when this question is put to them and in most cases their employer would be shocked by the response.

Work satisfaction surveys are now common in many organizations and the Human Resources profession has developed a range of surveys that can provide you with excellent feedback and suggestions for improvement.

Some Staff Satisfaction Tips.

1. Employ happy, go-getter employees. Do not poison the work environment by employing negative employees. Also employ staff who have a high level of emotional intelligence.
2. Provide open and honest leadership
3. Show support, appreciation and keep criticism to a minimum.
4. Thank staff for the work they do.
5. Secure staff that has a propensity to be adaptable and to learn.
6. Embrace key moments and symbols that inspire the above.

There is nothing too scientific or earth-shattering about these. So to get the most out of employees it is important to have high fulfilment satisfaction levels in your staff. This will improve the practice profit and lead to a better workplace for all.

Dare I say it (as an accountant) but the lack of sensitivity to staff satisfaction and quality largely stems from worn but doggedly persistent ideas on where to save costs in the practice. It has often been said that accountants 'know the cost of everything and the value of nothing'. And they (we) often control the cost and value trade-off decisions.

A gentleman by the name of Al Dunlap (not an accountant) had a nickname of 'Chainsaw' because of his profit at any cost approach to management especially through reducing staff numbers. Many large companies and employees would still be suffering because of the advice of this man in the 1980's and 1990s'. The damage was extensive. An extreme example perhaps but serious damage can still be done through decisions of much less importance. Staff want to have pride in their work and the practice they work for. If that is missing it simply becomes a work-to-rule job and motivation is quickly lost. Over many years I facilitated "Young Guns" meetings for up and coming young accountants and they made it very clear to me that they want to be noticed in positive ways, they want to be appreciated and they especially want to hear the two words 'thank you' when they do something well. We humans want to know we matter, that we are loved by someone and we feel safe.

Ring the Bell for Service

Generally speaking too, a firm's indifference to staff satisfaction and quality issues will be vividly on public display. In addition to speaking to the receptionist one only has to walk through an office to see whether there is pride in appearance, presentation and office layout. I have lost count of the many professional offices I have visited but one stands out in my memory. An appointment had been made with me to visit a two-partner country firm. Upon arrival at the scheduled time I found no one at the reception but there was a bell on the counter and a sign indicating "ring the bell for service." It was a while before a young lady arrived and she astonished me when she advised that the partner was not ready yet because he was still enjoying his midday nap! No doubt he was working on his life balance! After half an hour of waiting and a chance to observe the waiting area I noticed very old, outdated furniture, piles of National Geographic magazines that were decades old (and no other reading material); the young lady did not hang around – presumably she had important matters to attend to ; stark barren walls; no windows; and a great deal of dust. Eventually I was ushered into the partner's office where he was awakening from slumber with his feet, in socks, still on the desk. Clearly his time had come and within six months I was able to negotiate his succession and retirement – the reason for his initial contact with me. Although he was ready for retirement his practice was far from being 'investor ready' and he probably achieved about one-half of the potential selling price available for his share of the practice. Decades of cost cutting and reductions in quality had cost him dearly upon his retirement.

I have seen quite the opposite in country towns as well. I was called to a small town of just 4,000 people and was expecting to see something similar to the above. When I arrived I was shocked to find a two story very modern building with 110 staff and a very successful multi-disciplinary practice involving law, accounting, finance, financial planning and much more. A very highly professional firm…quality was evident. To my amazement they pointed across the road to an almost identical firm in an even bigger office with 140 staff! These two firms had been in tough competition for around 80 years as each pursued high quality and the local and extended community were clear winners. Professional services had become a major industry for this small town because of the drive and commitment to high quality.

Help Yourself to Coca Cola!

As an accountant I encourage diligent efforts to save money…I'm certainly not recommending cost blowouts. I do have difficulty however with partners/principals who try to save money on the wrong things, for example, cutting out biscuits in the staff room. I recall one memorable example. I was involved in the restructuring of a firm where one partner was effectively buying out his three partners (all were ready for succession/ retirement).

The task of implementing action with new systems, processes and stronger delegation was immense. For this to take place successfully it was vital to have staff on side and enthusiastic but motivation was clearly lacking. It was during a discussion with a senior staff member that he commented that staff (about 35) were very upset that their soft drink supply had been taken away from them! Upon further investigation I discovered that one of the retired partners, for many years, had stocked the boardroom fridge with coke for himself and an instruction to a support person to keep it stocked.

A staff member decided that it was alright to take an occasional bottle or can and others quickly picked up what was happening to the point, over years, where all staff were helping themselves in the belief that this was approved. The now retired partner had no idea this was happening because he took no notice of expenses…that was someone else's responsibility! The now sole practitioner who had taken over was a very careful man and soon discovered that he was paying over $10,000 per annum for purchases of Coca Cola…he immediately 'canned'(sorry…I couldn't help myself!) the purchases. Staff interpreted this as having lost a perk of the job and were very upset. My recommendation to the principal was to immediately explain truthfully to staff what had happened and reinstate the soft drink purchases, with limits, in recognition of 'the fantastic team of people they are' and as a 'thanks' for their diligent efforts in moving through these changes.

Look Professional

A quality mindset is the cornerstone of a quality firm and the costs of implementing a quality mindset are usually trivial – especially when the value to be obtained is considered. Be careful not to disable a quality mindset...if this happens, soon everything is going downhill – performance, productivity and quality. I am convinced too that a necessary condition to being professional is to look professional (unlike the practitioner mentioned above with his midday naps!). I don't just mean the appearance and dress of your people and your office environment, but especially whatever one is working on...the work we do for our clients. Tom Peters, a well-known author and management expert, suggests that when you see lots of coffee stains on the airliner's upholstery, start worrying about the engines. People, whether they are clients or staff, are definitely affected by their surroundings and the way they are treated.

Returning now to the very first line in this chapter ... the services we offer our clients, whatever profession you belong to, is the focal point for purpose and achievement. Many professionals and, in particular my own profession, are 'solution finders' and take much pride in finding the answer to the particular challenge that has been placed before you. Many practitioners are sometimes guilty of moving in and out of interviews with clients and taking one phone call after another with a priority of providing solutions as fast as possible and moving on to the next client. It has taken me too many years to realize that the art of listening carefully to the client is so important and all too often an undeveloped skill of professionals. Professionals, in the main, are excellent at building relationships with their clients, and without realizing it they are 'selling' their skills. It just comes naturally for most professionals and the professional would generally be horrified at the thought that they might be a salesperson but in reality that is an important part of the process. The client develops confidence in the ability of the professional to meet their particular need, however, I believe that it is fair to say that many professionals have not fully developed their listening skills to properly identify their client's needs…the focus being upon the immediate problem at hand.

In recent years I have found a very useful 'tool' that does have widespread use with sales people but not widely understood by professionals even though it has strong application. I refer to the book 'SPIN selling' by Neil Rackham. Now don't jump to the wrong conclusion, as I did initially i.e. that this book is probably about tricks, having the right pitch and so on. It is about the acronym of **S..P..I..N** which comes from **S**ituation? **P**roblems? **I**mplications? **N**eeds? These four questions or stages are each important and one must avoid the temptation to jump in with a solution (a habit I have found very hard to break). The first stage involves questioning your client about their current situation and giving them ample time to explain. The Good Lord gave us two ears and one mouth for a reason…so that we could listen twice as much as we speak. Inevitably you will find out a lot more about your client and the simple act of listening carefully will build your relationship with your client. The second stage involves questioning the client about problems, difficulties or dissatisfaction. Your client has a clear opportunity to state the problems. List them down. I have found another 'tool' very useful for this exercise and I use it often. I refer to Mind Mapping (invented by Tony Buzan) and again I refer you to his book and software that is in my assessment an amazing tool. The third stage involves questions to the client seeking answers as to the implications, effects or consequences of the problems already identified. Assist the client to clarify these perhaps in monetary terms or health terms, etc. and again list them. The final stage involves questions about the value or importance of a solution, i.e. needs. Again list these. With all of this information you can then show how you can meet explicit needs.

If your entire firm maintains such a focus it will become very apparent just what services you should be focusing you priorities on.

The SPIN tool helps you to develop the next step and that is a 'One-Page' plan. The following is a simple template that I have used more times than I can count:

DISATISFACTION Problems/ Isuues/ Now		VISION Need/ solution/where
• • • •	**Client Name**	• • • •
STRATEGIES	IMPLEMENTATION ACTION PLANS	TIMING Who & When

On the following page is an example from an actual workshop consisting of 60 staff and partners of an accounting firm. The name of the client of the accounting firm of course has been changed but it was a real client and as you can see there is strong focus on the services we should be providing this client. The fees under the 'Where' column are very much on-the-spot estimates but attention has now been drawn to the fact that there is much to be done for this client and if all services are approved then there is a total fee here in the order of $141,000 but more especially we have a very good base to hold some serious heart to heart conversations with your client. This workshop example did not have the benefit of the SPIN process.

NOW	Bloggs & Co	WHERE
Started in a garage in 2001 Supplying supermarkets $20 million turnover $1 million profit Mum & Dad (60's) - now son involved All compliance Reactive Financial controller in place **Current Fees $50,000**		**Est Fee** Div 7 A problems $10,000 Withdrawing funds - trust & Coy. $25,000 Training for son- Management $5,000 Succession planning $10,000 Competitor analysis $5,000 Strategic planning - business plan $8,500 A disaster plan $3,000 Audit on quality control/systems review $2,500 Waste Audit $3,000 OHS Audit $5,000 HR plan / strategies $1,000 Staff training $6,000 Choice of Super $1,000 Audit for Investor Ready $6,000 **Total Additional Potential Fees $91,000**

STRATEGIES	ACTION PLANS	TIMING Who & When By
Draft a presentation		
Analyse the 'where'		

My recommendation is that you identify your "A" clients first and then work towards completion of a one-page plan for each individual client. When these are finalized you will have a most comprehensive list of services that are in demand by your clients and I would be surprised if you don't substantially increase your practice turnover.

All of this, as well as clarifying your focus on your client needs, also help you to answer the question, "What business am I in?" A dentist might assume that since his business purpose is apparent, he only needs to advertise in the yellow pages in order to have a successful business, but having a website describing various dental problems and procedures could mean the difference between having a small practice and a large practice; dentists are in the information business as much as they are in the business of dentistry. I have come across a dental firm that advertises that they are in the "smile" business! You could be the best solicitor in your area, but if you and your staff don't demonstrate sensitivity to your clients' emotional needs, you might be sending them to another solicitor who can make them feel good even if they lose; a solicitor primarily practices law, but her secondary function is counselling. In our very rapidly changing world what was once a secondary offering or support service could become your primary business over time, if you are paying attention to market cues, but if you still make decisions based on an outdated definition of your business, they won't be aligned with its realities, and it will suffer. Many businesses today are finding it necessary to reinvent themselves in order to compete. It is increasing unlikely in today's highly competitive world that you can be all things to all people. Many sole practitioners attempt to be 'all things' in a one-stop shop for their clients but this is fraught with danger not the least of which is how do you maintain the knowledge and skills necessary and what impact does this have on your ability to delegate tasks and grow your practice. Clarify what your strength is, focus on that service and build systems and processes around that so that you can delegate to trained staff.

CHAPTER SUMMARY

- The services we offer our clients, whatever profession you belong to, is the focal point for purpose and achievement.

- If I had a dollar for every time I have heard the statement "Why can't we get good staff these days?" I would be a very wealthy man. In many practices the divide between principals or partners and staff has become highly polarized. I have actually been part of a major firm where your level or position in the firm determined which floor of the building you worked in …starting with partners on the top floor. Turnover of staff at this firm was over 30% per annum…one guess why!

- Generally speaking too, a firm's indifference to staff satisfaction and quality issues will be vividly on public display. In addition to speaking to the receptionist one only has to walk through an office to see whether there is pride in appearance, presentation and office layout.

- A quality mindset is the cornerstone of a quality firm and the costs of implementing a quality mindset are usually trivial – especially when the value to be obtained is considered. Be careful not to disable a quality mindset…if this happens, soon everything is going downhill – performance, productivity and quality. I am convinced too that a necessary condition to being professional is to look professional.

- Professionals, in the main, are excellent at building relationships with their clients, and without realizing it they are 'selling' their skills. It just comes naturally for most professionals and the professional would generally be horrified at the thought that they might be a salesperson but in reality that is an important part of the process.

CHAPTER 7
SYSTEMS, PROCESSES AND PROCEDURES

It is quite ironic, in my experience, that accounting practitioners who are usually considered to be the best advisors for professional business management are often the last to adapt good software systems to their practices. Again, the issue inevitably comes back to cost rather than value. Of course there are many exceptions to this highly generic statement and as I was preparing these notes I received a call from a sole practitioner who was seeking my assistance. In recent years he has been very quick to introduce the latest software and IT generally and he has reached a point where mid-year he and his staff have completed their full-year program because of the efficiencies that have been gained. He sought help to grow his practice through securing new clients.

It has also been quite disturbing to find so many accounting practices that maintain remarkably high levels of what is usually referred to as 'cash lock up', i.e. combined debtors and work-in-progress balances... often over six months and I have seen over twelve months (of normal annual turnover)! Many take out extra borrowing from banks to finance this investment, often at the very high overdraft rates required. If they had good systems and processes in place this investment could be reduced substantially to free up the cash to invest in better information technology and vastly improved systems.

Any examination of improvement to systems and procedures should always start with the client. What are the clients' needs first and foremost and how are we going to best meet those needs? This is obvious but in reality not carried out. Numerous surveys, for example, of the accounting profession for which I am most familiar, have been consistent over decades in highlighting the fact that the accountant is a most trusted advisor but there has also been a consistent negative response in these surveys that highlight the failure of practitioners to return calls, not being available, unwilling or unable to provide entrepreneurial experience and support in their advice, being too busy and similar.

Few professionals have any understanding of the need, for continuous improvement in their systems and procedures, to be constantly seeking out the means to improve the service provided and to improve awareness of client needs. It is not at all unusual, as already mentioned in this book, to find silos in practices where the head of the silo, the partner, principal or manager, has his or her own unique way of completing assignments and with staff holding yet further independent and unique ideas as to how to complete an assignment. I often hear it said "but David we must have professional independence and flexibility". I'm not arguing with that but I am saying that people can work faster, more efficiently, when they share the same methodology or planning and problem-solving framework. While different approaches may work well and no doubt produce different solutions, the important thing in a disciplined practice is that everyone uses the same approach. People can get on with the task quickly. Teamwork goes up and costs go down. They can check each other's work and pick up where others leave off without having to double-check what has already been done. New staff can be trained and become productive much more efficiently.

There should be ongoing questioning as to whether the process is properly defined? Is it working? I have already referred to the 'Sacred

Cows'...do we follow a process because it is reliable, efficient and meets the client's needs or do we do something 'Because that's the way it's always been done around here'. The more clear your processes and procedures the greater the opportunity to delegate tasks and release your higher skilled, talented people for greater responsibility and productivity.

Project Teams

I often strike resistance from professionals, who point out to me, 'But I am extremely busy...who is going to carry out this task of improvement and besides it will affect our productivity?' I am not suggesting that we should become too complex about all of this. I often utilize project teams.

Large corporations use highly organized project teams as an ongoing process and may even have full-time Project Managers to ensure that meetings are held and projects completed. I came across an accounting firm of six partners and about 50-60 staff that had 13 permanent committees established. These committees covered a range of issues from tax updates and audit standards to firm presentation and marketing and uniforms. I am not making that recommendation but interestingly, it did work for that particular firm. My recommendation is to keep things simple. A small project team of about 4-5 people with a specific timeline and a specific project brief. The team meets for an hour a week over eight weeks and at commencement elects its own chairperson and reporter (for all notes). Each week the team discusses and analyses the issue as follows:

> **First week** – Project Brief: ensure that there is a clear overview of the project and written in simple terms; what are the specific outcomes we are seeking.

Second week – complete a diagnostic of our present position.

Third week – the vision- what the outcomes should be at the end of the eight weeks.

Fourth week – how are we going to achieve this? What information do we need?

Fifth week – draft the plan.

Sixth week – develop solutions.

Seventh week – design a presentation to management with recommendations.

Eighth week – practice the presentation – you are selling your ideas – management needs to be convinced.

Your first project team might be, for example, to consider whether we should establish an intranet system with an online manual of processes and procedures and if so how do we go about doing this. Try to make the project team enjoyable – introduce some fun. I recall one team where the above was its project and it was nicknamed the 'chardonnay' team by the firm because they always met late on Friday and enjoyed drinking glasses of wine (or a beer) at the end of their busy week whilst addressing this issue. Another met over the lunch break once per week with Kentucky Fried Chicken, etc. brought in for them. Whatever motivations you use try to ensure that everyone is in agreement. If a partner or principal is involved I suggest that he or she take a back seat and try to let the rest of the team come up with the ideas and suggestions.

Depending upon the size of your firm you could have a few project teams running at any given time. If your firm is very small perhaps only one team operates from time to time.

Delegation and Encouragement

It is also vital that partners or principals provide encouragement and guidance. I encountered one firm… a five partner firm with around 45 staff…where the very first project team was established and after much prodding and cajoling a report was very hesitantly presented by the team to partners. Partners immediately took control, extensively criticized the report and were highly negative in their response. They spent much time drilling down to effectively produce their own report. Subsequently it was almost impossible to secure volunteers for further project teams.

The whole point of this exercise is that partners and principals do not normally have the time to devote to issues and if any progress is to be gained then it is absolutely necessary to delegate and to do so in an atmosphere of encouragement. It was also apparent in this firm that partners over a period of years had been quite intimidating and negative towards staff, mostly without realizing it themselves. Training in the soft skills or EQ was non-existent and there was an expectation of a high quality result in the belief that EQ skills came naturally somehow or were learned on the job. This was and still is a very high quality firm – due to a very direct participation in every assignment by partners but they have effectively created a rod for their own backs. The workload on partners is immense and the strain and tension is showing. The practice is growing at a steady rate with at least three partners needing to consider succession arrangements. Existing senior staff does not want partnership. Sooner or later the various pressure points will give way unless training is approached in a much more serious manner and delegation (not abdication) becomes part of a new culture of encouragement and support.

Training Cost

Quite some years ago the Australian Federal Government recognized that skills development was imperative to growth of the economy and introduced a compulsory 'Training Guarantee Levy'. It was introduced to raise the staff training efforts of Australian enterprises. Surveys had shown that many enterprises had no training at all and many more provided only minimal training. This legislation was drafted to encourage employers to spend between 1.5% and 5% of their annual payroll turnover on training. The legislation was abandoned when it was realized that government enforced rules were not working. Nevertheless there was much discussion and debate by experts and in my view the percentages determined are good indicators of a guide as to what should be spent on training. These figures did not include on-the-job training or 'lost opportunity' cost. These were direct actual outlays.

We will consider in more detail the training issue in another chapter.

DuPont Analysis

During my career stretching over more than 45 years I have witnessed enormous gains in the improvement of systems and procedures and there is now a bewildering variety of software programs available to all professions, all with the purpose of making your life easier. The cost v. benefit analysis is usually quite straightforward and yet there are still professionals who delay or hold back on decisions to take advantage of these tools. Very detailed manuals with step by step instructions are now available on intranet, i.e. your own private network for you and your staff, and this lends itself to huge efficiency gains. One simple example: in a world of formulae and finance there is one calculation that stands out above all of the rest and that is DuPont Analysis, developed in the 1920's (so it has now been around for nearly 100 years!) by the DuPont Corporation and calculates –

- Operating efficiency (measured by profit margin)
- Asset use efficiency (measured by asset turnover)
- Financial leverage (measured by equity multiplier)

In my youth I learned how to attend to the calculations manually and I found that the calculations were quite time-consuming because of the reiteration process involved. Computers have now reduced these calculations to mere seconds and the value of the projections that are possible is quite simply immense. And yet, as I often speak at practitioner conferences for accountants and financial planners I take the opportunity to ask for a show of hands as to how many in the room use this software, the numbers are always minimal and in one instance with approximately 300-400 in attendance only ten hands were raised! I cannot fathom why financial advisors would not take advantage of such a tool. I am reliably informed that in Australia most of the big banks use this tool…it would be speaking the language of the banks to have that information available by accountants to clients…and yet?

The Office Management software available today is incredibly detailed and enables you to avoid re-inventing the wheel and as most are updated regularly this also ensures that your firm is meeting all statutory requirements such as in Human Resources, Occupational Health & Safety, harassment, industrial relations, technical updates and so on. Many software developers that I have spoken to have advised me that professionals are generally very difficult to deal with because they are usually so insistent that packaged software should be tailoured to the way they do things within their own office and this can add greatly to costs of implementation. Variations to the package can also complicate implementation and if your practice allows everyone in the practice to tailour to their individual requirements you are creating a nightmare situation that will inevitably prove very costly.

Implementing Software

My recommendation is to accept the package as provided, once you have completed thorough due diligence and chosen the most appropriate package for your firm, then appoint a 'champion of the cause' from within your staff or partnership who has sole authority to make changes to the original software and whose task it is to implement and monitor the establishment of the software. Inevitably you will have staff (and partners) who resist change so it must be made clear and in no uncertain terms that the success of the implementation, to the benefit of the firm overall, requires the full support and co-operation of everyone.

The firm should explain that having invested strongly in this software they will come down heavily on rogue staff or partners who do not utilize the software. Future growth and efficiency of the firm depends upon full co-operation (I have come across firms that have tongue-in-cheek, with a smile, referred to this 'champion of the cause' as the 'Office Nazi'- clearly the person appointed requires a strong, perhaps forceful personality who doesn't suffer fools gladly. A lion tamer would be good!). There is always some resistance to change and this must be taken head on. Remember the Sacred Cows...turn them into hamburgers!

New Developments – the Next Challenges

It is also quite evident now that the world of computing is rapidly moving towards what is described as 'Application Service Provider' (ASP) or 'Cloud Computing'. I am not an information technology expert but my layman's understanding of this is that all programs and support are provided by an independent provider so that you no longer need to purchase software programs or invest as heavily in hardware...in effect you rent the programs from a supplier. You make much greater use of the internet and when one considers just how quickly electronic funds transactions (EFT) and other use of the Web has taken the world by storm then you can begin to understand how quickly this new development will occur. I have found very strong resistance by professionals to this change because of their need for control over client records, concern as to confidentiality, concern as to risk of loss of documents and much more. A "control" focus is what has led to the decline of key institutional power because of failure to adapt, e.g., authority of mainstream media, trades hall, parliaments, banks, town halls, men's clubs and so on. Think "institutional"; think death of the organization! However, most professionals have adapted quite easily to electronic transactions through EFT, credit cards and similar and I suspect that it is inevitable that ASP or Cloud Computing will be the next challenge for professionals. Those who have adapted quickly to technology already in their firms will find the ease of transition to be a smooth one.

On this subject I also refer you to another 'must read' book titled "The World is Flat". This is an international bestselling book by Thomas Friedman that analyses globalization, primarily in the early 21st century. The title is a metaphor for viewing the world as a level playing field in terms of commerce, where all competitors have an equal opportunity. The book also refers to the perceptual shift required for countries, companies and individuals to remain competitive in a global market where historical and geographical divisions are becoming increasingly irrelevant. There is currently a strong move by corporations and professional firms to 'outsource' basic functions to India and other countries where wages are very substantially lower. This book addresses this issue in detail but again my observation would be that for most professionals this is highly controversial and there is much reluctance to consider outsourcing any of their activities. The challenge is that some

firms have commenced this type of outsourcing and I am aware of a firm in a small country town that claims enormous success. Now these claims are difficult to confirm but competitor firms in the same town are in a quandary. They are perplexed as to what action they should take…do they allow this competitor to continue to achieve the success claimed or do they take them head on and compete on a level playing field?
It is possible that in the not too distant future professionals will be forced to follow this outsourcing trend but like many professionals I am presently reserving my judgment. It is the outsourcing to another country that bothers me most and, although possibly a high profile exception rather than the norm, the scandals surrounding the 2011 Commonwealth Games held in India, the corruption, the lack of concern about deadlines, the non-payment to contractors after the Games and similar matters have all created strong reservations in my mind but I do think that we should investigate more seriously the concept of outsourcing within our own country or even between countries where cultures are not too different, for example Australia and New Zealand.

The war for talent is going to become more serious and access to good people is increasingly going to grow as an issue for us. I have seen very successful outsourcing within Australia and within New Zealand, for example, where a valuable, experienced staff member leaves the community because of circumstances outside their control such as spouse career change and family ill health. These people were able to continue to work for the relevant firm utilizing all available technology including intranet, webinars, Skype, etc. In one such case a senior manager of a firm in the southernmost part of the South Island of New Zealand moved to Auckland in the North Island when her husband transferred in his position and she continued to carry out her tasks from her new address. Another unusual case involved a young Chinese man who had settled in very well in a firm in a very small country town in Queensland and had proved his value to the firm. His father back home in China became ill and son was requested to return home. The young man continued to work online for the firm for as long as possible.

A prerequisite to successful outsourcing of this nature is very good software and standardized processes.

Blame Culture

Professional firms are at their most efficient when they have the right people doing the right work at the right time in the right way with the right support and resources. In other words the firm needs to ensure that the resources of the firm are being used to their maximum potential. It is not unusual to find a 'blame culture' resulting in people being unwilling to take responsibility and hiding mistakes. It is also not at all uncommon to find after a staff member, or even partner, has left the firm, mistakes come to light and sometimes these have very serious consequences.

These could have been avoided if they had been admitted when they occurred and this will only happen in an atmosphere of trust. Reduce attempts to blame people for mistakes and seek to develop an open culture which allows learning and development.

I suspect too that the 'blame culture' arises through viewing staff as a cost not a resource. Some professions properly maintain costing systems through time recording. I very strongly support this but these cost systems were originally intended to be a point of reference in determining the final fee not the only point of reference. The main point of reference should be the value of the task to the client and this should be negotiated and settled upon in advance with client expectations properly managed. There will always be clients who expect something for nothing or who will try to bargain with you. If you rely solely on cost of time as your reference point your firm will leave itself open to disputes and difficult negotiations because many clients will be suspicious that time may be recorded that doesn't truly relate to them and of course clients generally have difficulty understanding the extent of the work carried out.

The Right Balance

The challenge for us as professionals is to ensure that we have the right balance of the right people working at their correct level of expertise. We have all seen highly trained, experienced skilled people carrying out duties that trained staff at lower cost rates per hour could have completed just as efficiently. Many of us would be guilty of this ourselves from time to time. People are a resource rather than a cost and it is up to us as employers to ensure that they have all the best resources that we can provide and that includes check lists, systems and procedures to guide them when there is room for doubt. The problem we often encounter is not that our staff doesn't work; the problem is that they're doing the wrong work.

If a hamburger business can become one of the most successful businesses in the world through systematizing with very comprehensive processes surely professionals can too? I am of course talking about McDonalds and I have seen first-hand through their charity days called 'McHappy Days', where I have volunteered to help out, just how efficient these young people can be. I have also witnessed three of my children learn how to successfully work in a business at very young ages – one became a McDonald's store manager at the age of 17; another at the age of 16 won the Crewman of the Year Award and his prize was a trip on the Young Endeavour ship that he learned to sail. This is Australia's sail training flagship and after his trip when I inquired of him "what was the one thing you learned that really stood out? His answer was "Dad, if I can do this I can do anything"...and he has moved on in his career to prove that, as have the others.

McDonald's processes are finally tuned to the 'nth' degree with temperatures and timing set to perfection and even a squirt of tomato sauce or slice of cucumber measured. They actually record and measure any waste. Sure, being a professional is far removed from making hamburgers...or is it? If McDonald's can train very young people to work a highly successful business with high quality, can't we?

"That Isn't My Job"

I have seen a large number of firms that have become very good at fire fighting but wouldn't it be better if we could see the smoke before the house burns down? Very few are good at fire prevention that's boring. They are good at fire fighting because they get lots of practice! Make the service to the client the primary focus not the individual's job. I have witnessed many, many times a discussion as to why a certain task wasn't carried out for a client, to hear the disappointing response..."but that isn't my job". Structure your firm so that everyone has a service orientation, not a job orientation. It can be too easy to watch a firm grow with large 'teams' handling functions with staff blissfully unaware of how well the firm was carrying out its responsibilities to clients – usually that is viewed as being a partner/principal responsibility.

The solution may be found in establishing small teams. Decentralize your practice and empower your people. In many practices I have changed the description "manager" to "client manager" to emphasize the change. Most firms have good software that allocates clients in the database to Partners/Principals who have the responsibility for full management of the client. Change this description as well to "Engagement Partner/Principal" because now we are seeking to delegate full responsibility for management to a team headed up by a 'client manager'. Client allocations in total value would not normally be equal but rather based upon their ability to manage a team in the true sense of the word 'manage'. This would normally be someone with good EQ skills, not just good IQ skills. You may have a manager who is quite capable of managing $1 million in fees revenue (or more). Your budget will determine how many staff is required, in this instance, possibly ten, including the client manager, or less (working on say $100,000 revenue per person). Another 'client manager' might have total revenue value of $250,000 and no staff because it is recognized that this person's skills in managing people are not yet where they ought to be but the person is quite capable of managing particular clients or a particular class of clients.

In the case of the 'client manager' with 9-10 staff I would be inclined to break that up into two teams under the supervision of that person. Create focal points of ownership, objectivity and obligation. Make them accountable. Each team leader should be responsible for supervision in every sense of the word. This includes training, counseling and regular evaluation. The team leader must have real authority …not just cheerleading and that leader becomes the focal point for accountability. I very much like the Balanced Scorecard approach to accountability and management and I highly recommend the use of this process. A recent Google of the words 'Balanced Scorecard' produced 2.1 million hits and you will find a wealth of information from the internet to assist you.

Tailoring and simplification of the process is required for professional firms and I have found that it can be relatively simple to implement. Start with partners/principals and work with these in the first year to ensure that it is fully understood and any bugs removed before implementing with teams. The Balanced Scorecard must be synchronized with your Business Plan and strategies so ensure that your firm goals are very clear before embarking upon this path.

Role Descriptions

An area that has not been handled well by professionals generally is the use of written role descriptions. Tasks are all too often expected of individuals without clear direction and how they are expected to work, behave and collaborate. Role descriptions are essential. Role descriptions are required for recruitment as well so that you and the applicants can understand the role. A role description defines a person's role and accountability. Without a role description it is simply not possible for a person to properly commit to, or be held accountable for, a role.

The process of writing role descriptions is actually quite easy and straight-forward. Many people tend to start off with a list of 20-30 tasks, which is fine as a start, but this needs refining to far fewer points, around 8-12 is the ideal.

Smaller firms commonly require staff and managers to cover a wider or more mixed range of responsibilities than in larger firms (for example, the 'office manager' role can comprise financial, HR, WIP and/or debtors control, scheduling and other duties). Therefore in smaller firms, role descriptions might necessarily contain a greater number of listed responsibilities, perhaps 15-16. Whatever the circumstances, the number of responsibilities should not exceed this, or the role description becomes unwieldy and ineffective.

Any role description containing 20-30 tasks is actually more like a part of an operational manual, which serves a different purpose. Role descriptions should refer to the operational manual, or to 'agreed procedures', rather than include the detail of the tasks in the job description. If you include task detail in a role description you will need to change it when the task detail changes, as it will often do. What would you rather change, 100 job descriptions or one operational manual? Similarly, lengthy details of health and safety procedures should not be included in a role description. Instead put them into a health and safety manual, and then simply refer to this in the role description. Again, when your health and safety procedure changes, would you rather change 100 job descriptions or just one health and safety manual?

Just working through the process with a staff member can be very revealing. I recall many years ago requesting a senior, experienced manager to assist me in the task of preparing role descriptions for the practice and I requested her to start with her own role. It took her quite a while and when she came to me with the final product I was shocked. She had produced no more than a half-page of description that was most substantially below my own expectations. She was a partner designate and I had great difficulty understanding the fact that she viewed her role in such a limiting fashion. It gave me very serious doubts as to her possible promotion. Who was at fault here? Whilst there was clearly fault from her perspective the exercise did strongly highlight the fact that my expectations had not been communicated adequately. She really did not fully understand her role but had high expectations. Some serious discussion took place after this and this lady today runs her own successful practice and I have no doubt that if I was to make the same request of her today there would be no misunderstanding

It is not at all uncommon for partners/principals to allocate assignments to staff without clear instructions or with inadequate information. The more detailed the instructions and information the less likelihood of inefficiencies and whereas partners/ principals often believe that there is a cost saving in reduced time 'on the slate' in the long run that saving will be lost if there is follow up-required, errors made through confusion and wrong assumptions as well as double handling. Far better to have a system in place that ensures that instructions are very clear and detailed.

Measure Publicly

Role descriptions are vital but only part of the equation if we are to ensure a service focus not just a job focus. Goals, measurement, comparison and feedback are all required. So put up a scoreboard in each team's work area. Work out goals with full team member participation and then measure publicly against those goals. Tie these to service…ensure the emphasis is always upon the client. Keep these measures as few, and as simple and straightforward as possible. The overall objective is not to create competition between teams but rather to provide visibility and objectivity for each team to judge its own service by relevant benchmarks. The feedback should go to the workers direct – again, all too often computer reports and so on usually go to partners/ principals first and do not find their way to the staff. It must become their service, their outputs, their obligation, and their rewards for achievement.

Client Managers

Give each of your client manager's genuine power. I recall very clearly the first time I was involved in a change of structure to set up the client manager teams. Partners in our firm had been for many years the persons fully and utterly responsible for every decision or task on a client and silos were the modus operandi with many partners knowing little or nothing about staff in silos other than their own. When the decision was made for this change of structure it was also determined that clients would be allocated to the new client managers across the firm with the result that former managers and supervisors now were receiving directions from not just one partner but six! Partners of course retained their 'engagement partner' role. The new 'client managers' reacted not unexpectedly pointing out that if they had, in an extreme situation, six partners come to them in the one day , all demanding urgent action and priority they were in a 'no win' position. It was carefully pointed out to them that they were in no different a position to that of an engagement partner, who in an extreme example had six clients come to them in one day and make the same demand. What was required was an exercise of negotiation and managing expectations. Communication in these situations is paramount and leadership skills are developed. It took time and 'yes' problems did arise but skills developed and the firm grew quickly. Extra staff training is required with the opportunity for all staff to have input and to make suggestions for improvement.

Client Coordinator

In recent years we have also seen the introduction and use of a person sometimes titled a 'client coordinator'. The client coordinator acts as the face of the firm for the clients. This person interacts with the client on a day to day basis in a pleasant manner and handles queries and issues effectively and efficiently. This person is responsible for client interaction and follows up all matters until completion. The managing of client expectations and regular communication can change the perception of your firm overnight. Most clients are reasonable people and if you treat them fairly and keep them informed you are unlikely to have any negative reaction. If there is information missing for completion of the assignment this person does the follow-up work directly with the client. This person could also check information delivered by clients. I remember a case where a client delivered a CD containing the year's transactions and other information to an accounting firm. No one checked the CD and it was placed in storage pending commencement of the assignment. Three months later when the person responsible picked up the information to commence the task the disk was found to be blank! An interim fee had been rendered.

Manage Expectations

In my workshops I have often used the example of my local Ford dealer where I have had my cars serviced over many years and I have noted an outstanding improvement in service. In years gone by they had a chalk notice board at the small, crowded reception area that advised their various prices and invariably when you collected the car there was some 'unexpected' repair that turned up with its extra cost. Today each customer's car goes under a serious scrutiny with a computer diagnostic and up the hoist for inspection whilst you wait and observe. As items are discovered they are explained and you are handed a check list and prices agreed upon before you leave. Even after this it is still possible that something else will be discovered during the service and they now phone you as soon as it is discovered to advise you whether it needs urgent attention, price and so on. Many dealers now send a survey form after every service so that customers may praise or criticize any aspect or any person – how many professionals do that or are prepared to? They leave nothing to chance and yet time and time again I hear of accounting firms for example where the accountant completing the work discovers that, say, there is a mistake in the information provided, perhaps the bank reconciliation doesn't reconcile, and rather than phone the client to give the client the option to take the records back and rectify them, the accountant takes extra time and fee to rectify the matter and argue the fee with the client later. A much stronger, relationship with the client is available through a quick phone call to the client (perhaps by the client coordinator) explaining what has happened and that the firm is prepared to attend to the rectification (with an estimate of the extra fee) or offering the client the option to fix the matter.

Mistakes

I have used examples of a hamburger business and a mechanic business to emphasize that focus on a customer or client through good systems, processes and policies is available to all businesses and we as professionals should be the leaders not followers. The corporate/ commercial world has advanced rapidly in business management techniques whereas, very generically speaking, the professional world has not kept pace. For example, 'six sigma' when entered into Google produced 12.5 million hits and yet I have never seen the concept applied in professional firms. "Sigma" in this case is a statistical term used to describe how close a product, or in our case a service, comes to meeting its quality goal. One sigma means 69 percent of services are acceptable; three sigma means 99.7 percent, and six sigma means one is achieving process perfection 99.9999997 percent of the time. Translated, that's only 3.4 mistakes per million.

I recall not so many years ago a local Australian airline was losing my luggage every time I flew with them. When I wrote to them to complain they responded with what was clearly a standard reply letter advising that they handled multimillion items of luggage and the losses they incurred amounted to only 1.25% of the total and they considered that this was an acceptable rate. For me the loss rate was around 100% and I wrote back to inquire whether their error rate of 1.25% was applied throughout their organization in which case do they consider an error rate of 1.25% acceptable for flight landings! I received a more detailed response and an undertaking to take more personal attention to my luggage…which I think they did because the losses dropped right off after that.

In the case of professional firms there probably is an acceptable error level. There certainly is a material consideration and it is more likely these days that accountants for example would not seek to reconcile a bank account to the cent or maybe even to the nearest $10 or $100. I would hope that brain surgeons have a nil error rate! I suspect that most professionals would not be measuring to this extent but I do know that in the accounting profession, if write-offs or deficiencies are any indication, the error rate is unacceptably too high. I have seen write-offs as high as 40% pa. The average is around 4-8% pa. Write-offs in this context refer to the amount written off the recorded value of work in progress.

It is not my intention here to go into a detailed explanation of 'six sigma' but rather to highlight the fact that there are methodologies, tools and software that assist greatly in managing any professional firm. Over the years I have accumulated over 500 tools and processes that are useful. The truth is that I have no more than ten favourites that I use most of the time. Again, simply typing in the words 'tools and processes for professionals' into Google produces over 7 million hits! Another 'must read' book for professionals is "The Consultant's Tool Kit" edited by Mel Silberman. This book provides details of guides and diagnostics, many of which may be downloaded from websites and they are free. With so much help available one can only wonder about professional firms that do not have good management systems, processes and procedures.

Centralism

I do find it disturbing that in Australia and many other countries governments seem intent on moving to greater centralism...hospitals, schools, councils. Centralism proved to be a massive failure in the Soviet Union. This country was the world's prime and most devoted practitioner of centralism for three-quarters of the twentieth century, and its citizens have paid a terrible price for the experience. Will we ever learn? Professional practitioners too should take note at the micro level and understand that the same principles apply. Centralistic management stifles innovation and creative outlook and across the western world we are just now beginning to realize that staff commitment is inversely proportional to the degree of centralized management and control. The more you tighten the screws by management the more your people will resist. If you want commitment you have to involve them in your processes and decisions and organize small to win big.

The Possible Solutions

Quite a few years ago I tried an experiment that worked amazingly well. Leveraging of staff numbers is a great way to improve your income but, of course to do this successfully staff must know what their role is, be competent to do it and have clear instructions and very good systems and processes to work with. In the early days of making the changes I found that my 'open door' policy for staff queries was taking up more and more of my time so I introduced an instruction to my people that, before walking into my office, they were required to carry out some research in relation to the matter under query and only then come to me with three possible solutions and their recommendation as to the solution they thought was best. There was also an office policy to never assume anything because that can make an 'ass' out of 'u' and 'me'... assume! If in doubt check it out...if still in doubt be sure to make a note in the work papers for the Reviewer's attention? Over time the result was truly remarkable. It was possibly one of the greatest confidence building steps I could have taken with my people. Gradually the frequency in interruptions in my office dropped off and at the same time confidence of the staff increased as they saw more and more that the answers from their research were proving to be correct. Base all of your actions on trust and respect until the scoreboard and other measurements show that intrusion is required. There will inevitably be staff whose skills are simply not up to the task.

I am not advocating that you should 'just let go' or 'get out of the way'. That is abdication as distinct from delegation. You do have to walk the talk yourself and help find the way, show the way, and pave the way. I have often had the argument put to me ... "But it is much quicker to obtain an answer direct from you and that surely is a cost saving for the client because less time is going into the work-in-progress records through the timesheet?" In the short run the answer is "True" but in the long run you are creating a rod for the back of the partner/principal/ manager that has a growing line of people waiting at the door and the staff member is not learning the deeper implications and detail relating to the query. A quick answer from a senior shortcuts the learning experience and longer term development for the individual staff. This is also leadership training and creating good leaders below you do not push you out, it pushes you up. And this leads us into the subject of chapter 9....Leadership.

CHAPTER SUMMARY

- Any examination of improvement to systems and procedures should always start with the client. What are the clients' needs first and foremost and how are we going to best meet those needs?

- Few professionals have any understanding of the need, for continuous improvement in their systems and procedures, to be constantly seeking out the means to improve the service provided and to improve awareness of client needs. It is not at all unusual to find silos in practices where the head of the silo, the partner, principal or manager, has his or her own unique way of completing assignments and with staff holding yet further independent and unique ideas as to how to complete an assignment.

- People can work faster, more efficiently, when they share the same methodology or planning and problem-solving framework. While different approaches may work well and no doubt produce different solutions, the important thing in a disciplined practice is that everyone uses the same approach. People can get on with the task quickly. Teamwork goes up and costs go down.

- Project teams - my recommendation is to keep things simple. A small project team of about 4-5 people with a specific timeline and a specific project brief. The team meets for an hour a week over eight weeks and at commencement elects its own chairperson and reporter (for all notes).

- Partners and principals do not normally have the time to devote to issues and if any progress is to be gained then it is absolutely necessary to delegate and to do so in an atmosphere of encouragement.

- Australian Federal Government legislation was drafted to encourage employers to spend between 1.5% and 5% of their annual payroll turnover on training. The legislation was abandoned when it was realized that government enforced rules were not working Nevertheless there was much discussion and debate by experts and in my view the percentages determined are good indicators of a guide as to what should be spent on training.

- I often speak at practitioner conferences for accountants and financial planners and I take the opportunity to ask for a show of hands as to how many in the room use DuPont Analysis software, the numbers are always minimal and in one instance with approximately 300-400 in attendance only ten hands were raised! I cannot fathom why financial advisors would not take advantage of such a tool.

- Appoint a 'champion of the cause' from within your staff or partnership who has sole authority to make changes to the original software and whose task it is to implement and monitor the establishment of the software.

- Most professionals have adapted quite easily to electronic transactions through EFT, credit cards and similar and I suspect that it is inevitable that ASP or Cloud Computing will be the next challenge for professionals. Those who have adapted quickly to technology already in their firms will find the ease of transition to be a smooth one.

- Professional firms are at their most efficient when they have the right people doing the right work at the right time in the right way with the right support and resources. In other words the firm needs to ensure that the resources of the firm are being used to their maximum potential. It is not unusual to find a 'blame culture' resulting in people being unwilling to take responsibility and hiding mistakes.

- The challenge for us as professionals is to ensure that we have the right balance of the right people working at their correct level of expertise. We have all seen highly trained, experienced skilled people carrying out duties that trained staff at lower cost rates per hour could have completed just as efficiently.

- I have seen a large number of firms that have become very good at fire fighting but wouldn't it be better if we could see the smoke before the house burns down? Very few are good at fire prevention that's boring. They are good at fire fighting because they get lots of practice! Make the service to the client the primary focus not the individual's job.

- An area that has not been handled well by professionals generally is the use of written role descriptions. Tasks are all too often expected of individuals without clear direction and how they are expected to work, behave and collaborate. Role descriptions are essential.

- Goals, measurement, comparison and feedback are all required. So put up a scoreboard in each team's work area. Work out goals with full team member participation and then measure publicly against those goals. Tie these to service… ensure the emphasis is always upon the client.

- The client coordinator acts as the face of the firm for the clients. This person interacts with the client on a day to day basis in a pleasant manner and handles queries and issues effectively and efficiently. This person is responsible for client interaction and follows up all matters until completion.

- Across the western world we are just now beginning to realize that staff commitment is inversely proportional to the degree of centralized management and control. The more you tighten the screws by management the more your people will resist.

- The possible solutions - I introduced an instruction to my people that, before walking into my office, they were required to carry out some research in relation to the matter under query and only then come to me with three possible solutions and their recommendation as to the solution they thought was best.

- You should 'just let go' or 'get out of the way'. That is abdication as distinct from delegation. You do have to walk the talk yourself and help find the way, show the way, and pave the way.

CHAPTER 8
BENCHMARKING

Let's face it! A book written by an accountant for professional service firms – including accounting firms – simply could not be written without a chapter on benchmarking. Accountants love spreadsheets. When I commenced the establishment of networks of accounting firms around 20 years ago I was in a sense pioneering the concept of independent firms working together and benchmarking between independent firms was a key to the success of these networks . Really all I was doing though was continuing with a practice that I had already been carrying out as a managing partner in an office within a 'Big 4' accounting firm where comparison figures between offices of that firm were very regularly scrutinized very thoroughly and discussed in depth. If an office achieved an outstanding result everyone wanted to know how they did it? If an office achieved a poor result everyone wanted to know why and what could be done to rectify the situation?

Prior to each of these network meetings my organization contacted each member requesting completion of an Excel template that provided basic details for the member firm. From that information comparison schedules were then prepared and needless to say when we came together the detailed scrutiny by all of these accountants in the room was really quite remarkable to witness and over time these comparison sheets became more and more detailed. The firms that achieved higher-than-average outcomes were the subject of serious questioning…how did you do it? What changes did you make? And so on. There can be little doubt that the member firms of these various networks we chaired and facilitated obtained very great value from this simple exercise of looking outside their own firm to see how they compared with firms similar to their own. This was an exercise in continuous improvement and over the years these member firms can look back with much pride in the enormous gains that they achieved.

Key Data - Examples

As time wore on this exercise became more and more detailed and just some of the key data included :

- Months Debtors
- Months WIP
- Cash 'lock up' (being the total of the above two)
- Fees per Principal
- Fees per staff (including partners)
- Write offs/Deficiency %
- Net Profit per Principal
- Average rate achieved per practice hour (all staff & partners)
- Average rate per chargeable hour
- Productivity % (firm overall)
- Staff per Principal
- Average fee per client
- Number of hours worked per principal
- Principal's Average Utilization
- Net Profit per Principal per Hour
- Return on Investment %

....to name only a few!

Some Examples of Non-financial Data

And of course these are all financial and now in an era of Balanced Scorecard and similar measurement many more non-financial benchmarks may be added including for example

- Job turnaround time,
- Your firm's % rating in ongoing surveys for 'delighting' clients,
- Your firm's success rate in securing your profile identification of ideal clients,
- The number of culled clients this month,
- The number and value of clients now on fixed pricing/ value pricing,
- The extent of completion of courses and training that have been tailoured to staff and partner needs arising from regular skills audits,
- Staff turnover,
- Staff appraisals / reviews completed,
- Lost clients

…once again, just to name a few.

Best Practice

Benchmarking is really a search for industry or profession best practices that lead to superior quality. Many practitioners attempt to achieve this through reading professional journals, newsletters and books. They attend conferences and seminars listening to expert speakers. The listen to CD's in their cars and on their iPods. By far and away the best approach however is the direct contact with other independent firms that are actually achieving what you hope to achieve. Fundamentally what we are doing is learning something new and the challenge is to implement these ideas into our practice.

Benefits

The benefits from benchmarking can be huge in terms of improvements to processes such as client service delivery and time taken to complete assignments.

Over a great many years we have identified just some of the benefits of benchmarking as follows:

- Improved understanding of our internal processes and systems and business practices;
- Establishment of key success factors and true measures of productivity;
- New ideas leading either to continuous improvement or break-through change;
- Improvement in understanding and meeting the needs of our clients;
- A view of external conditions leading to the establishment of more relevant goals and strategies;
- Becoming more competitive in the marketplace;
- Becoming aware of and emulating industry/profession best practices.

Still Room for Improvement.

Nevertheless even with this sort of scrutiny and benefits I still see much room for improvement. It is my view that we should also look outside our industry or profession and learn from the corporate world and other sectors of business. One very large accounting firm that I was involved with set themselves some rather interesting strategies and goals as part of their 5 year plan but the one that really caught my attention was the goal to achieve 24 hour turnaround for their compliance assignments… at a time when the average turnaround time was around three months! Incredible stuff but they were convinced it was achievable. Their thinking was to tap into the offshore/outsourcing resources available through countries such as India, Malaysia and Vietnam. Their thinking wasn't so much because of the price advantages but for the turnaround time. In effect they saw the possibility of a 24/7 operation for their practice.

Whilst local staff were sleeping and resting staff in different time zones could still be working on these compliance tasks to produce completed assignments in much reduced time…and ultimately pleasing their clients.

Also with the aim of increased assignment turnaround time perhaps we should look to the processes used in businesses such as McDonalds or Domino's Pizzas to examine how they process their 'products' so quickly …and even give guarantees if they are not fast enough! Sure they are totally different products/ services but are the processes and systems really all that different in terms of the objective – to please our clients or customers? Perhaps we may only pick up one or two points to assist us but that may just give us the edge over our competitors.

Are we the Last Bastion of Resistance to Change?

There are so many tools now utilized in the world of commerce that many professionals would have no idea even as to their existence. I often get the feeling that in so many ways professional service practitioners are the last bastion of resistance to real change. Some of these tools include:

- Dupont Analysis
- Many marvellous new software products in forecasting – one most recent that has caught my attention and, as an accountant, I like very much is called Castaway. Go to www. castawayforecasting.com .
- Balanced Scorecard.
- Six Sigma
- On line software that manages your HR tasks and payroll.
- Business & Strategic Planning software.
- Marketing and promotion software and support.

- Client categorization.
- Mind mapping.
- SPIN.
- Surveys (1000's)
- Skills audits
- Forcefield analysis
- Life balance tools.
- Project teams.
- Strategic SWOT
- Waste audits
- Cause and effect.
- Competitor Analysis
- Continuous Improvement.
- Change Formulae – D X V X P
- 5 Whys
- Gap Analysis
- Pareto Principle
- Rule of 72
- PDCA
- Product Portfolio Analysis

…the list is endless and new 'tools' are being added every day. This list is just the small tip of a very large iceberg! I suspect that a Google search would produce hits in the millions. Yet , how many professional service practitioners would know of even just a handful of the items in the above list?

Reach outside your immediate profession and practice and ascertain what is happening in our wider world. The point of reference from which quality or excellence is measured for your firm may be found there to give you a distinct winning edge over your competitors and enable you to achieve growth in your practice beyond your wildest dreams. The truth is that much of the benchmarking activity we see in the professional service firms is at a very low level of intensity and not very sophisticated in many cases. As time moves on more and more of these tools will become available and you need to be alert to their development and ready to use them.

For a very comprehensive coverage of this subject you would be well-advised to go to http://davidparmenter.com/ . David is considered to be the 'King of KPI's' and has much in-depth commentary in his website and books. His work on KPIs has received international recognition.

CHAPTER SUMMARY

- There can be little doubt that the member firms of these various networks we chaired and facilitated obtained very great value from this simple exercise of looking outside their own firm to see how they compared with firms similar to their own.

- Benchmarking is really a search for industry or profession best practices that lead to superior quality. Fundamentally what we are doing is learning something new and the challenge is to implement these ideas into our practice.

- The benefits from benchmarking can be huge in terms of improvements to processes such as client service delivery and time taken to complete assignments.

- One very large accounting firm that I was involved with set themselves some rather interesting strategies and goals as part of their 5 year plan but the one that really caught my attention was the goal to achieve 24 hour turnaround for their compliance assignments…at a time when the average turnaround time was around three months! Incredible stuff but they were convinced it was achievable.

- I often get the feeling that in so many ways professional service practitioners are the last bastion of resistance to real change.

- Reach outside your immediate profession and practice and ascertain what is happening in our wider world. The point of reference from which quality or excellence is measured for your firm may be found there to give you a distinct winning edge over your competitors and enable you to achieve growth in your practice beyond your wildest dreams.

CHAPTER 9
LEADERSHIP

Leadership has been described as the "process of social influence in which one person can enlist the aid and support of others in the accomplishment of a common task". Definitions more inclusive of followers have also emerged. Alan Keith of Genentech states that, "Leadership is ultimately about creating a way for people to contribute to making something extraordinary happen." According to Ken "SKC" Ogbonnia, "effective leader-ship is the ability to successfully integrate and maximize available resources within the internal and external environment for the attainment of organisational or societal goals."... from Wikipedia.

To this we could possibly add that it is also about achieving something which otherwise would not have been so positive, or effective, or sustainable....or not at all.

You will note from a reading of this definition and others that leadership is not management and the question one often has to address in professional firms is "Who in fact is in charge around here?". I've often heard it said... "Who is the first amongst equals?" The first challenge in many professional firms is to try to find out who is in charge.

I have sat in on more partner meetings than I care to count and inevitably it becomes apparent that all in attendance believe that as owners and partners they are all equal and therefore entitled to a say in every decision of the firm. This can become very unwieldy and earlier in this book I discussed the role confusion in wearing three hats and the example of the receptionist's chair. Many professionals see their responsibility to their clients as paramount and delegate or, perhaps more accurately, abdicate all matters relating to management to someone else…usually an administration or support type person who is more often than not, inadequately trained for the role and lacking the authority to do a great deal.

One very quick test - If you're seeking an important decision and the person you're dealing with says "I'll take this to a partners meeting/Board for discussion" - you are dealing with the wrong person.

Good Leadership

Leadership is rarely considered to be an important role in professional firms and if a person is a nominated leader that person is usually expected to maintain the same duties and level of productivity as was the case before the appointment. The result is that leadership fails to be addressed as seriously as it should. You can't run on autopilot with people charting their own directions and taking their own initiatives and yet that is precisely what is happening in a great many firms. You cannot be a leader unless you understand what leadership is all about. All too often being appointed leader of a professional practice is viewed as being akin to receiving the Sword of Damocles and "heavy hangs the head that wears the crown".

For most professionals their studies and training would have had little or no EQ training (or soft skills training). Any courses would have been almost entirely of a technical nature and many professionals have said to me over the years… "I didn't learn anything about managing, motivating, and leading people". Often the wrong sort of person altogether is elected to leadership because of a lack of understanding as to the requirements of a good leader and as a result we tend to see more prima donna personalities running professional firms. Sometimes the leadership is simply handed on to the person considered to be next in line by way of age or years in the job!

Good leaders are consistent in their advice that:
1. You need leadership to be successful; and
2. You won't have it unless you empower people to exercise it.

Obviously some decisions can only be made at the very top – but they should be the exception, not the norm. The leaders at the top should chart the course, not constantly steer the ship. For this reason when I facilitate a Strategic Planning workshop I start with the partners so that the 'owners' clarify in their own minds, together, what they are trying to achieve…just what is their vision? After this we then sit with our staff and present a draft plan to them for their views, feedback and commitment. I have often been most pleasantly surprised by the issues raised at staff 'retreats' that partners have completely overlooked! In one instance, for example, staff in a country town firm raised the issue that they loved living in their town and working for their firm but, although correspondence study worked well, to advance their career they had to leave to go to a city university or college. The partners were stunned when they realized that about eight of their senior people were in this position. A strategy was determined to open a branch office in the nearest city with the main purpose of transferring work to that office to keep their staff whilst they attended the university or college.

Leadership Training

It has not been uncommon in my experience to work with a firm in clarifying a marvellous vision – truly inspiring stuff – only to find later that they did nothing with it! A vision without execution is a hallucination.

Values should flow from the top down; decisions flow from the bottom up. That implies that everyone should have leadership training and development. The sad fact is that very few professional firms share that view and staff are all too often viewed as a cost rather than a resource. Knowledge and skills development are vital to the health of an organization. According to a Merrill Lynch study, Motorola estimated that every dollar spent on training yielded $30 in productivity gains within three years. That's thirty times! Whilst surfing the net recently I came across an outstanding report produced by IBM titled 'The Value of Training'. Go to this website to view this valuable document: https://www-304.ibm.com/.../ibm_white_paper-value_of_training.pdf. It also refers to research in relation to the cost of doing nothing!

As someone who has worked with many hundreds of professional firms I am convinced that there are no poor firms, just poor leaders. It is also wrong to assume that leaders are naturally born. Leaders have to learn the necessary skills. They must be taught and a major skill to be acquired is how to motivate and to accept personal responsibility for building a common purpose or vision. Many or most Baby Boomer professionals have had little or no training in leadership and currently retain leadership positions and the mantra is "I learned through the School of Hard Knocks and so can they!" and it is very difficult to convince them of the value of training. For many years I facilitated "Young Guns" conferences for up-and-coming young accountants often identified as potential partners. The enthusiasm and excitement at these meetings had to be seen to be believed. One particular presenter that I used was Dr. Lanning Sowden. He worked in universities for years both in Australia and overseas. Today he has his own consultancy business; he is a Registered Psychologist, a Chartered Member of the Australian Human Resources Institute, an Accredited Practitioner with the Australian Institute of Training and Development, and member of the Australian College of Clinical Psychologists. Lanning has worked with some of the largest corporations in the world helping them develop their people. With this sort of experience and these qualifications you can understand that this man had some idea as to what he was talking about. His sessions were incredibly lively, full of action, and a great learning experience – for me as well as the attendees! These "Young Guns" always left our sessions with specific action plans to complete, high on adrenalin, and enthusiasm that needed bottling and yet invariably when I followed up to see how they were going, I was told that their boss didn't want to know and showed no support and as a direct result that enthusiasm and commitment was quickly lost! Thankfully the tide is turning and there are many young people today who are actively seeking out employers who will provide them with EQ/soft skills training. They understand the value of good training as an investment in their own future.

Employer From Hell!

I was recently on a panel at the end of a national conference of account-ants and a sole practitioner in the audience stood up and proceeded to complain quite derisively and with unrestrained ridicule his experiences in employing Generation Y staff. As he put it "I put a lot of my time into training these young people and they leave within three years and I have lost a huge investment in terms of lost opportunity cost". A few quick questions from me revealed that there was no formal training. Training was, as he described it, 'on-the-job-training'; there was little if any feedback given to the staff member – feedback was more likely to be of a negative nature; and absolutely no program of long term development. As he spoke one could quickly assess that he was most likely an employer from hell and it was surprising that he managed to keep these young people for as long as three years. There was a very strong expectation that because they had a degree (obtained at their own time and expense) they should hit the ground running knowing what to do from Day One and be profitable immediately. The truth of the matter of course in this day and age is that a degree is an indicator of IQ not EQ and the real training in soft skills usually only begins when they commence employment. It was highly unlikely that this man 'walked the talk' in terms of any values and his leadership skills were clearly lacking.

Attitude

There is a talent war today and Australia with its very low birth rate like so many other western world countries is unlikely to see this 'war' easing anytime in the near future. As a direct result we are not always going to be able to secure the best people as quickly as we would like for our team and this is where training becomes so much more vital. I do believe that if you find people with the right attitude you can train them for anything. I recall a newspaper item about a legal firm with a photograph of five women – all of them had started in the firm as a receptionist and each had studied and eventually become an associate of the firm. When I address staff at Retreats I often relate this story and tell them that "each of you has the potential to become partner in this firm if you want to".
It is up to the leader to instill confidence, enthusiasm, opportunity and commitment to give that individual the drive and determination to make it happen.

A lost Dogs Home!

A two-partner firm, with about 30 staff in a small country town, approached me with a genuine concern that they had not been carrying out regular performance appraisals of staff. In fact they were so busy they hadn't completed any appraisals for some years. They inquired whether I might be willing to carry out individual interviews and report back to partners with recommendations that might arise from this exercise. I explained that I couldn't do performance appraisals because quite obviously I didn't know the staff and their abilities or roles.

Nevertheless I established a process with templates including a SWOT for each person to complete, a short list of crucial questions aimed at generating discussion by the individual and I offered to each person to make a note anonymously of any suggestions or criticisms of the firm they might have. Each interview was limited to one hour. This proved to be one of the most positive assignments I have ever had! To a person they were full of praise for their bosses. This little country town, many miles from city life had been experiencing tough times through drought, closure of local industries and more. What this firm had done was that whenever anyone approached them for a position they went out of their way to find a position and train them for a role. Many were spouses of farmers experiencing very tough financial times. As one staff member explained to me "This place is like a lost dogs home, we're all made to feel so welcome and treated like family". Whilst I was there one lady came to me and said, "I'm not supposed to tell you this but look at what I just received? This is why we love this place so much." She was going overseas next day having been selected as part of a community choir and the partners had provided her with "an extra something …a cheque for a large sum (to her) just to help out a bit towards your expenses". Needless to say she was thrilled by the gesture. And of course it should not have surprised me when I walked into the Boardroom of this firm to see a magnificent corner bar, well stocked with liquor and supplies – this unit was a recent Christmas gift from all of the staff to the partners! Have you ever heard of anything like that?

This practice, during difficult economic times, was recording excellent growth and a net profit that was amongst the best I have seen. The two partners are men of very good character with very high values and quite obviously a belief that you treat everyone as equals. They walk the talk and the esteem and respect, with which they are held, not just within the office but also within the local community, is second to none. This firm didn't need formal appraisals – they knew every day how people were performing because they communicated with them in friendly positive terms all the time – seeking their input, complimenting them when a job was well done, encouraging them. I doubt that I have ever seen a more loyal group of people.

Contrast this with the same size firm I mentioned earlier in this book where staff in a Retreat for the firm identified 75 issues of concern – most of which related to communication. Partners in this second firm quite simply did not communicate (in a positive way) with their people. This firm experienced perennial problems securing staff and constantly complained that they could not find good people.

Engaging Employees – the Statistics

Research has found that engaging your employees has never been more important than in the current environment of skills shortages and global war for talent. Many surveys have now revealed that the majority of people feel under-valued and under-utilized in their workplace. Highly engaged employees outperform disengaged counterparts by up to 28%. The improvement on your bottom line can be up to 57% greater. And then you have the additional challenges of high staff turnover and costs of recruitment where you have disengaged staff. Again Research (from the Mercer Survey of Australia at Work) shows nearly 25 per cent of Australian employees will change jobs this year. And when you consider staff turnover costs are up to 150 per cent of a person's annual salary it's obvious why staff retention is quickly becoming a burning management priority. The figures from the Mercer survey are valid, but some experts argue that they are only the tip of the iceberg. Professional firms need to factor in the costs of decreased productivity, lost investment in training and development, loss of revenue for key sales or management executives, administration set up, equipment purchase, recruitment costs, the new employee's induction into the firm's culture, management downtime in interviewing candidates, legal fees and payout commitments. There can be a lot more to staff turnover costs than first meets the eye, which is why it's so important to recruit the right candidate first off and then do what you can to keep them challenged, satisfied and engaged. When all of this is taken into account one begins to understand the true value of a good leader to a professional practice. Effective communication starts at the top.

Seven Initiatives

How Do You Keep Employees Happy, Motivated and Engaged with the Firm?

Here are seven practical initiatives you can take to help keep your staff happy, motivated and recognized:

- **Listen to your people** - make your employees feel you are interested in them personally.
- **Reward and Recognise** - build your employees' esteem. Show them you value their opinion and ideas and that you're watching their performance. Sometimes a simple monthly 'Star Performer' Award handed out by a Partner in front of co-workers can have a far greater impact on motivation and retention than any financial reward.
- **Career development** - prepare career development planning

strategies for individual employees that align with each employee's needs and desire for future growth. It may mean keeping certifications up to date, sending employees to seminars, or just providing subscriptions to magazines and journals. Whatever the effort you make to help this person's career it will long be remembered.

• **Provide challenges** - employees should be given new job assignments to keep them alert and challenged. What better reason to stay with a company than to snare a new job or client assignment? Providing employees with challenge and excitement can encourage them to stay; they don't want to risk missing a good opportunity.

• **Work/life balance** - consider providing staff with the flexibility to achieve a satisfactory mix of time at home and on the job. Perhaps offer reduced working hours or work-from-home options, where possible. The French, for example, have adopted a 35-hour working week as a mandatory part of society, and employees are reporting a better work-life balance as a result. The message? Long hours and satisfied employees rarely mix.

• **Salary Watch** - McKinsey's and other recent research studies confirm what management gurus have maintained for decades: as long as salary is in the general range for a particular role, most employees will not consider it the deciding factor in job satisfaction. So, check to see you are paying at an appropriate level. And consider creative salary options that align with the individual's own needs such as childcare, gym memberships and 'work from home' days.

• **Mentors** - partner inexperienced and experienced workers together so both can benefit from the other person's knowledge. The experienced worker may impart technical skills, for example, while the new person may bring social/cultural lessons to the relationship.

Leaders v. Managers

I believe too that many professionals do not understand that there is a difference between leadership and management and I quite like the following summary of different mindsets from the book "The Five Pillars of TQM' by Bill Creech (another 'must read'!):

Leaders shape the outputs	*Managers chase the inputs*
Leaders focus on services	*Managers focus on individual jobs*
Leaders encourage new ideas	*Managers enforce the old ideas*
Leaders stimulate right things	*Managers monitor for wrong things*
Leaders thrive on tough competition	*Managers talk little of competition*
Leaders prize comparison with others	*Managers see scant need for comparisons*
Leaders think of involvement programs	*Managers think of suggestion programs*
Leaders empower others to make decisions	*Managers tightly control the decision process*
Leaders see leading as animate and proactive	*Managers see managing as inanimate and reactive*
Leaders think of a dynamic, caring human system	*Managers think of a business following a script.*
Leaders think of improving initiative and innovation	*Managers think of improving compliance and conformance*
Leaders shape organization character, culture and climate	*Managers assume that neither a big deal- nor their job.*
Leaders provide the vision	*Managers carry it out*
Leaders make it better	*Managers make it run*
Leaders make it happen	*Managers hope it happens*
Leaders create more leaders	*Managers create more managers*

As I carefully read each of these I couldn't help wondering if at various times I have wandered and wavered my way through all of these! Bill does continue in his book to indicate that he doesn't think that everyone should fit a perfect profile of one or the other. He is basically suggesting that these distinctions provide markers of what to look for. We could no doubt add a column to each of these with a 0-10 scale and assess ourselves with a total score….now does that make me a leader or a manager? …proactive!…comparisons!…new ideas! I do believe though that this exercise does provide excellent assistance in helping us to determine whether we are 'leaders' or 'managers' and/or to assess our current 'leader'. It would be an interesting exercise to request all personnel at a firm retreat to make a 0-10 rating of the current leadership and then add up the grand total of the team. It might also be a bit too revealing! Do we really want to know! An interesting challenge don't you think?

I'm sure many readers have come across the 'mushroom principle' of management, i.e. 'keep your subordinates in the dark and feed them lots of …fertilizer!' There is also the 'seagull manager' who 'flies in makes a lot of noise, leaves… a mess…on everyone and flies out again' (you will note that I have been careful in choosing my words here).There is also the frog manager who jumps from lily pad to lily pad without making an impression anywhere. We do have a lot of fun with our managers don't we but the truth is that a good manager is worth weight in gold. What we are really trying to do in this section is draw a distinction between a leader and a manager and understand that good leadership is vital to success of any professional practice.

The issue of control is something we should not gloss over. I have often heard accountants described as 'control freaks' and that's possibly true of many professions. Professionals must maintain an eye for detail and a slip up, especially in the case of say a brain surgeon or an airline pilot is something we really do not want to contemplate. Hindsight is a truly marvellous skill isn't it? It is with the benefit of hindsight that I can now see that, 'yes', I was a control freak…and perhaps I still am (ask my wife!). But maintaining control is a 'manager' mindset and I am now highly embarrassed when I think back to some of the decisions I made as a 'partner-in-charge' or 'managing partner' of a firm. I recall instructing our Office Manager to make sure that the 4 drawer cabinets in her room and her office door were locked at all times when she was out of the room. My thinking was that the financial information and other particulars for our firm were highly confidential and without proper security could get into the 'wrong hands'.

What wrong hands? Consider the message I must have sent out to the team at that time about trust? It certainly would not have been a message that stimulated them or encouraged them to take ownership. They were key stakeholders in the business even though not direct owners.

True Profit

Now I most strongly recommend that firms produce their figures in true profit terms and that means include realistic commercial salaries for partners, interest on monies advanced to the business and so on. Most professional firms do not produce their financial accounts in this way and the 'net profit' is effectively inflated because it does not recognize these realistic expenses. It is prudent of course to maintain 'control' over payroll records and details of salaries and other payments to individuals including partners.

I have come across a sole practitioner with about 25 staff who producers an annual glossy report with a summary of the firm's financials and a lot of non-financial information about staff, business successes and so on. The net profit, after allowing for commercial salary, market interest and other items to him has never exceeded 10% and he uses that as a motivator for the firm to help them to understand that we have to improve. By the way Goodwill should be re-valued to market value every year and interest calculated on that 'investment' as well. All of this information in a glossy report is presented in a professional manner at an annual meeting. He very truly sees his team as stakeholders in his practice and he has been very successful in securing their full involvement and commitment.

Partner Salary Calculations

There are many ways to calculate partner salaries and in the case of at least one 'Big 4' firm today almost everyone is described as a 'partner' from manager up! However there are at least four basic measures –

1. **Market:** what would that partner realistically generate as a salary in the open market? I recall in one workshop the sole practitioner put the question to his staff – to his absolute amazement they thought he could secure a commercial salary outside the practice of at least $300,000. They certainly valued his worth even if he didn't!

2. **Rule of thumb:** what are the large organisations using as a benchmark – the figure varies considerably but anecdotal feedback I have received suggests figures in the order of $120,000 - $150,000.

3. **Look at the current salary and current charge rate** of the highest paid staff member, e.g., say $60,000 and $150/hr. Then look at the partner current charge rate, say $200/hr. What we are

saying in these circumstances is that through charge rates we have assessed that partners have a premium of 33⅓% over the staff member therefore applying that same premium to partner salaries we would arrive at a salary of $80,000.

4. Most firms apply a multiple to professional staff salaries to arrive at the charge rate, i.e., 3 times, 4 times, etc. and therefore the fees turnover expected from that staff member as an individual. Use that same multiplier in reverse on partner personal generated fees, e.g. say $300,000 fees generated by the individual partner – divide that by the multiple, say, 3, in this instance salary would be $100,000.

A Scoreboard

Proper measurement systems are a must. Without meaningful comparison, people in all walks of life are simply not objective about their strengths and weaknesses. It is natural to try to overstate strengths and underestimate weaknesses. *"Facts stand wholly outside our gates; they are what they are, and no more; they know nothing about themselves. What is it then, that pronounces the judgment? Our own guide and ruler – Reason."* Marcus Aurelius, noble Roman and philosopher. You can't apply reason without facts and a great many professional firms make little or no effort to collect and analyse these facts. You can't pick the winners without a scoreboard and no one will know how to improve. It is necessary to get the competitive juices flowing. The aim is to encourage your staff to be thinkers for your firm not just doers for your clients. Be careful not to overdo this – managers come into their own on this, all too often introducing rules and regulations that stifle thinking to 'save us from our past mistakes'. The issue of monitoring productivity in accounting firms is a very good example. Staff become clock watchers, the 'six-minute' people, and lose sight of the value we are offering our clients. Everything is recorded in timesheets and these become the only means of billing clients. I am not advocating removing time sheets – this recording was established as a costing guide and that is how it should be utilized…as a guide only.

Employee attitudes are important so keep the measures simple and relevant. I have previously listed in this book, examples that I consider might be appropriate. Seek an answer to the question, "How are we doing?" The primary goal is to influence behavior, so keep this exercise as simple as possible and tie these measures to processes such as Balanced Scorecard.

Communication Illusion

Make sure the feedback loop is strong otherwise you have wasted your time. "The greatest problem in communication is the illusion that it has been accomplished", George Bernard Shaw. Maybe the greatest problem in leadership is the delusion of adequacy. All too often leaders feel that by making appropriate announcements or distributing an email the job is done. There are misunderstandings in communication every day. Recall my previous example of the firm with 75 issues – virtually all relating to communication. Show that you are serious about acting on this new information. A couple of good examples spring to mind here:

1. During World War I British soldiers in the trenches lost their field telephone and a sent word-of-mouth message "Send reinforcements, we are going to advance". The message at headquarters arrived as "Send three-and-fourpence; we are going to a dance."

2. During the dreadful 2011 Queensland floods a regional city recorded front page news of a local farmer who lost 9,000 pigs in the floods. The news spread internationally and a country

newspaper in England decided to check into this incredible loss and made direct contact with the farmer who explained, "No, no, no…9 sows and pigs!"

Our world abounds with messages that do not portray their original attention –

Some examples:

- During travels by car in Ireland at one stage I became totally lost and was relieved to arrive at a large roundabout with signs – the two council signs pointed in opposite directions to the same town!
- A notice in a hotel: "The manager has personally passed all the water served here."
- Sign in a hotel lobby: "The lift is being fixed for the next day. During that time we regret that you will be unbearable."
- A dry cleaner: "Drop your trousers here for best results."
- A Tokyo hotel: "You are invited to take advantage of the chambermaid."
- A Japanese hotel: "Cooles and Heates: if you want just condition of warm in your room, please control yourself."

Misunderstandings are inevitable. The secret to better communication: The harder you work at it the better it gets.

Just as if to compound the problem each profession has its own jargon or language and often firms, over time, develop their own separate jargon not generally understood by people outside the firm.

Bill Creech, author of "The Five Pillars of TQM" developed the following 25 keys to making our communication a language of purpose:

1. Speak the language of trust, not mistrust.
2. Don't confuse fancy words with profound ideas.

3. Don't harangue the many as the message for the few.

4. Reward the messengers of bad tidings, not shoot them.

5. Listen intently to the dissenting view; it may be right.

6. Keep all the language goals-directed, not rules-directed.

7. Talk in numbers as well as words to crystallize purpose.

8. On key issues communicate several layers deep.

9. If the policy is important, put it in writing - concisely.

10. Listen for the echoes to learn if it's all getting through.

11. Follow up to ensure there is full comprehension throughout.

12. Remove all barriers to upward communication.

13. Be candid and tell it like it is - without fear or favour.

14. Get all possible facts before expounding on the conclusions.

15. Get out the straight skinny – to combat misinterpretations.

16. Don't overhype or advertise. Let action speak the words.

17. Praising the winners has more power than criticizing losers.

18. Credibility depends on flexibility. Not mindless consistency.

19. Knowledge is power when widely shared, not withheld.

20. Feel free to admit you don't know, but you do want to learn.

21. The best opening sentence of all is: What do you think?

22. Listening, hearing, caring are the keys to make it thrive.

23. Provide the means and the incentives that will make it work.

24. Go where you need to go. Spend whatever is needed.

25. Treat the communications grid as an electrical grid. Any node failures leave people in the dark. Fill the vacuums. Find the reason they're there. Fix the grid.

…and overall I would add: Be prepared to say, "I don't know", "I was wrong", "I am sorry".

Change Resistance

I am often alarmed at that reticence of professional practitioners to implement change. In this incredibly fast moving world we live in delay will simply hold your firm back. All too often there is a conflict of interest on the part of individual partners to slow things down…perhaps retirement is just around the corner and there is a reluctance to outlay funds on new ideas; perhaps one, some or all partners own the building and do not want to see growth outpace capacity; perhaps a partner has needs for cash to educate children or pay off a mortgage and so seeks maximum draws of cash; and so on. There is glacial slowness in many firms to change. I agree very strongly with Tom Peters in an article in Business Watch titled "Nine Steps to Speeding Up Your Operations,"

> *Become a pioneer in the application of information technology, both inside and outside the firm. Inside the firm you have to link everyone together, across levels and functional barriers. All information must be available to virtually everybody in the organisation. The biggest problem is that you have to start now. You won't have time to catch up later. Many firms are waiting for industry standards to evolve. But that's not the point.*
> *About 95 per cent of the issues related to application of information technology are power and organization issues, not technology issues.*

My clients and business associates have seen me quote the following many, many times because it is a favourite and has so much truth:

> *"Some people in this world make things happen;*

Some people in this world watch things happen;
Some people in this world wonder what's happening"

Leadership Makes all of the Difference

To make things happen you must be competent, you must be active, you must be punctual, you must be unlimited and so on..........but what do you have to do to be competent, to be punctual, to be active, to be unlimited etc. You definitely have to invest your time but only time will not make all the stuff, you also have to spend hours of concentrated thinking so as to reinforce your investment to bring out the optimum output. I see so few practitioners willing and able to allocate time for this important work and many firms effectively have a culture that penalizes partners that do ...through productivity comparisons and other KPI's. All too often the 'leader' or managing partner is still expected to produce at the same level is prior to the appointment.

There are certainly a considerable number of people who just keep watching things happen and never do or make any achievement by themselves. These people are those who are limited by foolish thoughts and concepts and do not have a scratch of the mental attributes that mark the people who make things happen.
There are also yet other people who will not even keep themselves aware of the achievement of other's. They are certainly miles away to even reach par with the first category. Whenever I think of these people I recall the practitioner, mentioned earlier in this book, who had the bell to ring for service in his reception area and was enjoying his daily nap at his desk!

Some readers may have viewed episodes on TV of "Undercover Boss", a show I quite enjoy and over time you will have noticed that inevitably the show is about the boss relating to his employees in a very personal way, recognizing them as the individuals that they are and rewarding them for their commitment to the company. Of course they never show anyone other than committed personnel but the message is a very clear one and again, all too often, practitioners play a 'conversational ping pong' (referred to earlier in this book) with their employees and worse still, with their partners…never really getting to know the person and what makes that person tick or showing respect for that individual. How can practitioners ever hope to secure commitment if they do not make the effort to understand and know their people? A leader's vision too has only power to the extent that it is shared by those who are asked to carry it out.

Leadership does make all the difference …always. A leadership survey reported in HR Leader magazine in Australia in April 2011 reveals that "a staggering 49 per cent of Australian workers believe that their boss is not up to scratch." The report questioned 170,000 employees from Australia and New Zealand about the effectiveness of their leaders. The Aon Hewitt report found that only 51 per cent of workers said that they "agreed" or "strongly agreed" that their boss was an effective leader. A much earlier survey and report in Australia titled "Leadership in Australia" (sponsored by Telstra) attempted to identify the 'cultural imprint' of Australian workers, i.e. what makes Australians different? There were many quite revealing findings in this report but of specific interest to me were the following:

    • Recognition is important for Australians as for other cultures, but it should be sincere, perceived as well-deserved and low-key.

    • Communication is highly important, and receiving information is a reflection of trust.

• Australians expect to be told the truth and are generally prepared to face it but they also have well-developed sensors for detecting when someone is trying to pull the wool over their eyes. They have finely tuned "Bullshit Detectors" [sic].

• The most powerful way to motivate Australians is to give them a "cause" – something that transcends being the "biggest" or the "best", and has desirable social, moral, national or community associations.

I'm confident that these apply equally to any culture and the concept of well-developed sensors or "Bullshit Detectors" has developed as a counter to the growth in 'spin' advocated by way too many organizations.

A CEO of a major Australian Public Company once confided in me that their organization was undergoing intensive strategic planning and communication with their staff but "they had already determined the outcomes that they wanted and the exercise was merely to let them believe that they were involved." Many workers have become skeptical about their employers, especially generation 'Y' that is now the source of much consternation by companies who see this generation moving on too quickly if they are not happy in their work. They are now more focused on 'merit or value' of what the organization is doing, whether it is worthwhile, sustainable, "real", has integrity, etc. Perhaps they have learned lessons from watching their parents made redundant, often after lifetimes of commitment and dedication, and marched out the door under the guidance of a security person with cardboard box containing personal items!

Ben Palmer, CEO of Genos, recently commented that "Disengagement with leaders at work is a problem that is all too common in the Australian workforce. In our surveys, we find that there is a lot of dissatisfaction with management at the moment and I think that what many leaders don't realize is that it's this dissatisfaction that causes people to just come to work and clock on and clock off, and not feel motivated to put in the extra effort for their organization." He further commented, "There isn't a particular style of leadership that works best; instead you need to employ a much more individualized approach." Therein I believe lays the secret to success... "a much more individualized approach.". Respect the individual; acknowledge the individual; "do unto others what you would have done unto you".

Above all avoid the intimidator approach. Don't huff and puff over the wrong things; don't yell and scream at the wrong people. That's an exercise in futility and a sure way to ruin your firm.

A personal view and one I know is held by many of my professional associates is that we are presently experiencing a dumbing down in our schools. The expectations from schools, teachers, curriculum directors, etc. are way too low and there's insufficient involvement of many parents, in terms of expectations of their children. Students are increasingly falling prey to the "we're entitled" and "I have rights" mindset. Our schools have found ways to calibrate classroom instruction to a lowest common denominator. So how do you deal with this? The answer is in training with a special emphasis on EQ training and I refer you to my many previous comments in this book. Your focus, however, upon recruitment will now require much greater attention to ensure that you are employing people with the right attitude... people who are willing to learn. One of my associates has told me of a conversation he had with a US Baseball Coach and Recruiter who said he had stopped classing fantastically talented hitters and pitchers from South America, Mexico, etc. because they had such poor schooling and they didn't have capacity or appetite to learn new skills, complex game plays and similar. He said talent was a given, the capacity to learn and grow was now number one criteria.

You can no longer simply accept written CV's as a basis for assessment. Are you aware that there are actually courses now at TAFE Institutes and other centers of learning for preparation of CV's? I will never forget, having narrowed down to half a dozen applications for interview based upon written CV's, one applicant who presented remarkably well but I couldn't quite get to the bottom of what her real skills were so I put the question directly to her, "What do you think your best skill is?" and she answered, "Writing CV's!" I politely suggested that she was applying for the wrong job.

The world will belong to passionate, driven leaders, people who not only have enormous stocks of energy but who can energize those whom they lead.

CHAPTER SUMMARY

- Leadership is not management and the question one often has to address in professional firms is "Who in fact is in charge around here?". I've often heard it said… "Who is the first amongst equals?" The first challenge in many professional firms is to try to find out who is in charge.

- Many professionals see their responsibility to their clients as paramount and delegate or, perhaps more accurately, abdicate all matters relating to management to someone else… usually an administration or support type person who is more often than not, inadequately trained for the role and lacking the authority to do a great deal.

- Leadership is rarely considered to be an important role in professional firms and if a person is a nominated leader that person is usually expected to maintain the same duties and level of productivity as was the case before the appointment. The result is that leadership fails to be addressed as seriously as it should.

- Staff are all too often viewed as a cost rather than a resource. Knowledge and skills development are vital to the health of an organization. According to a Merrill Lynch study, Motorola estimated that every dollar spent on training yielded $30 in productivity gains within three years. That's thirty times!

- The employer from hell! There was a very strong expectation that because they had a degree (obtained at their own time and expense) they should hit the ground running knowing what to do from Day One and be profitable immediately.

- If you find people with the right attitude you can train them for anything. When I address staff at Retreats I often tell them that "each of you has the potential to become partner in this firm if you want to".

- Engaging your employees has never been more important than in the current environment of skills shortages and global war for talent. Many surveys have now revealed that the majority of people feel under-valued and under-utilized in their workplace.
- Seven practical initiatives to keep your employees happy, motivated and engaged with the firm.
- Leaders v. managers – there is a difference!
- Partner salary calculations – at least four basic measures.
- Proper measurement systems are a must. Without meaningful comparison, people in all walks of life are simply not objective about their strengths and weaknesses. It is natural to try to overstate strengths and underestimate weaknesses.
- Make sure the feedback loop is strong otherwise you have wasted your time. "The greatest problem in communication is the illusion that it has been accomplished", George Bernard Shaw. Misunderstandings are inevitable.
- All too often, practitioners play a 'conversational ping pong' with their employees and worse still, with their partners…never really getting to know the person and what makes that person tick or showing respect for that individual. How can practitioners ever hope to secure commitment if they do not make the effort to understand and know their people?

CHAPTER 10
CALLING IT QUITS

Some Crystal Ball Gazing!

- Succession within professional firms will reach a crisis point.
- Leadership voids will emerge as entrepreneurial autocratic firm founders retire.
- Firms will struggle to develop smart buy-out plans for retiring partners.
- Firms will be forced to make clear distinctions about the services they provide.
- Strategy will evolve around specialty services and expertise.

These are but a few of the predictions that some of the most prestigious and respected consultants are making for many professional firms. In particular, in 2008 the American Institute of Certified Public Accountants established a task force to examine this issue as part of its ongoing research and released a very comprehensive report. As a reader of this report I couldn't help but notice the use of the word 'distressing' as frequently applied to their findings. The report points out that "It is critical that practitioner's begin succession planning now in order to secure their firm's future." Creating a written succession plan is a prudent step yet from my experience very few firms do this and this report backs this up with actual percentages…as low as 9 per cent for sole practitioners. More often than not succession or exiting of a partner is handled in a matter of weeks rather than years and inevitably costly problems emerge.

Succession is emerging as a crisis problem now, and firms must address it in their current strategic plans. The reality right now however is that so few firms have formal succession plans or strategic plans.

The "Baby Boomer" wave that we have read and heard so much about is impacting on all professions now. Consider these facts:

- The eldest of the baby boomers turns 65 this year – many have already retired.

- Recent surveys highlight the fact that a very large proportion of professional practitioners are over 50.

- Currently 85% of current Tax Agents in Australia are male (per www.impactlists.com.au).

- A rapidly increasing number of graduates are female and to quote Pru Goward, a former Australian Federal Sex Discrimination Commissioner, "When they graduate from university they have other responsibilities, such as family formation and child rearing, and a biological clock that cannot be denied." With this outlook facing young women, and their partners, it is no wonder that women are demanding family-friendly work conditions such as part-time work and flexible hours.

- The young are entering the workforce later.

- Some professions have a poor image and are not attractive to the young.

- The young are more mobile.

- The size of the workforce in many countries is declining in real numbers.

Time is Critical

Practitioners and firms across the country have built businesses of value, but the majority have done nothing to ensure that value or even its continuity beyond it. In many cases, they may have worked 20 or

30 years to build a business that may end up being their most valuable asset. Many practitioners don't think beyond their own life in the business. Then, by nature, they're not able to build the kind of continuity in their practice that's critical for servicing clients in the future.
Ideally, the time to start thinking about succession planning is five years before you plan to retire. You need time to effectively get your practice 'investor ready' and to ensure that the transfer is orderly and not traumatic to your staff and clients.

You need time to think about your options. If you've spent 20 -30 years building your firm, you're not going to decide over the weekend what to do with it (although I do know of instances where this has happened!). There is much to be done in getting the 'financials' right, e.g., cash lock up, etc. You have to get a valuation of your firm. Then, you have to search for the right buyer (internally or externally), do your due diligence and negotiate a deal.

Obstacles

While, logically, succession planning should be about retirement and money, more often than that, it ends up being about death or disability. Look at the percentage of people who become disabled or die unexpectedly. You should be planning ahead to retire, and to extract some money from your business. It should be a positive experience. But, even if you're not thinking about retiring, you should still do succession planning. For many principals/partners their major asset is tied up in their practice and they do not believe that can retire because of:

- Insufficient retirement savings.
- Practice cannot do without them.
- No real successor.
- Client relationships.

- Debt disincentive for young 'partners'.
- Too sensitive to discuss.

The Global Financial Crisis in September 2008 did impact on the retirement plans of many practitioners especially when share values and property values took a significant hit and some of these practitioners deferred their retirement date pending recovery.

Consolidations and Corporatizations

Consolidations worldwide in all professions are still gathering steam and many are still gaining momentum in Australia under a different name or model. WHK is the best known accounting group in Australia and New Zealand and has proved to be most active in acquiring practices moving from being unknown to being the 5th largest accounting consolidation group in Australia in a relatively short period of time. Some have failed along the way, the most notable being Stockford Limited, another accounting firm consolidation, that in effect merged 53 firms in one day – listing day, on the Australian Stock Exchange. It failed relatively quickly and I am personally aware of many very sad stories that arose as a result. Many practitioners transferred their practices into the company in return for shares in this Public Company in the belief that they could sell their shares after an agreed time, realizing their value they had grown over many years. Unfortunately they didn't get the opportunity and the company went into receivership. Some were able to buy back their practices from the Receivers but the reality is that all suffered losses.

Businesses are moving into other businesses: banks have moved into in-surance, financial advice, investments, travel and it is my understanding that legal services and accounting services are under consideration if not already in place. GE has moved from electrics into finance. Management consultants move to where the dollars are

Practitioners who have no planning in place may well be encouraged to consider an exit by way of sale to a consolidator but great care must be taken – the traps for the unwary are many and every model is different requiring detailed due diligence. Some principals are simply unable to cope with the corporate world and the loss of authority that usually accompanies such a change. The story of the collapse of Stockford Ltd is a whole book of its own and there are countless versions as to why the company collapsed. Many would argue that it occurred because of circumstances outside the control of management.

Investor Ready

As part of the succession planning process I am a very strong advocate of being what I call "investor ready". I know that I have repeated this theme a few times in this book but I never cease to be amazed at the lack of preparation that firms put into this exercise knowing full well that any prospective buyer will of necessity usually carry out a very comprehensive due diligence. Yet time and time again I come across firms that do not have up to date financials (prepared on an accruals basis), no formal valuations, no budgets, no business plans, no profiles, and no policies and procedures manuals and so on. Even the relatively simple exercise of cleaning up the Balance Sheet and Profit & Loss Statement is so often overlooked and many Balance Sheets quite simply could not be described as anything other than a dog's breakfast! So many professionals seem to overlook the fact that this is an exercise in unlocking the true value of your firm and without preparation any prospective offers can only be at the lower end of the scale.

Many small firms are linking up with larger 'branded' firms retaining their independence for now but with an eventual sale or listing a clear intention when the timing is better. Merging of firms is also occurring at pace with 'economies of scale' often being the main benefit sought. However, in my view very few mergers actually work well. Most fail. The prime reason is the failure to identify the short window of opportunity to reconcile cultures. All too often it is totally overlooked and one of the parties eventually emerges as the stronger and more dominant party to impose its culture on the newly combined firm. Inevitably there will be dissension from the other party and very real challenges will emerge through lack of co-operation, undermining decisions and so on. Friction can grow to the point where a separation is ultimately required.

Fewer Owners

In future it is increasingly likely that commitments to pay retirement benefits will be made at the time of admission of a new partner rather than at a time closer to the retirement of the older partner. Older partners will sell new partners an interest in a practice upon admission, with payment due upon the older partner's retirement. Consequently, professional firms in the future probably will have fewer owners. Fewer people will want to take the risk of partnership. Those that do will be seeking larger fee bases and the model of the future (short-term) is likely to have a minimum $3 million per partner. This will also be made possible through vastly improved systems, procedures and training.

Firms that do not move quickly to this model are likely to be taken over or fall by the wayside. I have already found firms that have much higher leverage. A sole practitioner in Sydney working under the name "Bell Partners", for example, is reported in the 2010 BRW magazine Top 100 accounting firms as producing revenue in excess of $10 million with 69 staff and has expanded rapidly since.

Leadership

This has been covered extensively in the previous chapter but the professions will suffer a leadership void as the days of the autocratic founder/ managing partner disappear. A generation of managing partners who founded their firms have already commenced to retire. The autocratic, entrepreneurial founder tends to stay longer, and the longer he/she stays, the less likely the firm is to survive to the next generation. You can cause your firm's stagnation and demise by staying too long because it's hard to give up that power.

Training of selected partners for leadership and practice management will take on more importance. Few firms presently provide training in these areas. Informal networks, however, are currently providing the opportunity for these young partners or partners elect to experience 'real life' issues and practical experiences. These younger partners / managers are finding the opportunity within these networks to speak to other principals and managers, exchange ideas, share difficulties and generally find support and mentoring to help them to learn important lessons as quickly as possible.

Three Areas of Succession

Essentially there are three major issues to focus on:
- Client succession,
- Management and/or leadership succession and,
- Ownership succession.

Once the first two are addressed it's easier to sell your stake in the practice. Client continuity is an issue, because if your clients don't transfer, there's no business to transfer.

The second issue, management succession, addresses whether you've groomed partner level people who can ensure the continuity of the business. You need to make sure that the people who take it over are able to sustain it. You also have to look at the transferability of your practice. If you're ineffective as an operator of the practice, there isn't much to hold onto. The cash flow from the practice and the potential for client base to transfer are critical components.

Critical Questions

Some critical questions you need to ask about your practice:

1. Are you building a business or a book of business?

The first challenge to resolve is what you are building: a business or a book of business. A book of business is an asset that is entirely dependent on its owner to generate cash flow. There is usually significant attrition when sold, and the personal nature of it makes it difficult to transfer. A business is an enterprise that is systematized and less dependent on its owner for its success. By the nature of professional firms it is hard to reduce dependency on the owner completely, but the more one moves to a leveraged practice model, the easier it is to transfer and the more value the seller would receive.

Neither model is better than the other - it is a matter of personal choice. There is some intuitive appeal to plying your trade without having to invest the time, money and energy to build an infrastructure. But the consequences are diminished value and appeal to buyers.

In either case, it is prudent for most practitioners not to count the value of their practice as part of their retirement plan.

2. How long will the window of opportunity to sell practices remain open?

3. What is your time frame for making the transition?

4. What are your strategic alternatives (internal sale, external sale, merger, consolidation)?

5. What prospective buyers would be most compatible with your style and your clients (geographic and philosophic)?

6. What is the best approach to your best prospect?

7. What will the other party perceive as the strengths and weaknesses of your practice?

8. What are your deal killers (price, terms, and duration of agreement)?

Concentrating on building a highly profitable, easily transferable business with reduced dependency on the owner is the most important aspect to building value in a practice.

Benjamin Franklin said that nothing is certain in this world but death and taxes, and professional firms ought to be ready to deal with both eventualities if anybody is. Nevertheless, a surprising number of professional firms don't have a written succession plan to provide for continuation of the business after one of the owners withdraws or dies. For a small to midsize firm, such a plan is its only defense against potential legal, financial and personnel calamities when a senior partner leaves unexpectedly.

Advisers Need Good Advice Too!

The skills of succession planning are part of the professional currency of accountants-although practitioners apparently use them more on behalf of their clients than their own firms. More than three-quarters of those replying to a recent American poll said they didn't have a written succession plan in place and that the withdrawal, disability or sudden death of a partner would pose a significant challenge to their business Critical Issues to be considered:

• If an existing partnership – what does the partnership agreement provide? Many small partnerships have a standard partnership agreement or none at all which makes a firm vulnerable. Your solicitor should draft or review your partnership agreement with an eye to succession issues. Where the firm's structure is corporate, whether the impetus is death, disability or retirement, the key issue is buying out the withdrawing shareholder or partner's interest.

For a sole practitioner a practice continuation agreement is fundamental and is, in effect, a succession plan for that firm. This contractual arrangement with another practitioner or firm provides that in the event of death or disability, the party agrees to immediately take over the practice under a predetermined compensation formula and payment schedule. A spouse and/ or heirs as well as estate executors should be made aware of this agreement. It's a good idea for the practitioner to inform key clients too to be sure it is acceptable to them.

• Non-compete agreement.

• Buy-back provisions

• Representations and warranties.

• Indemnification.

• Performance of duties

• Payment terms.

• Security or collateral.

• Resolution of conflicts

• Interest rate on contract.

• Transferability of fees.

- Normal loss in transition: 5-10% of existing fees.
- Clawback arrangements.
- Part- time partners/ phase out.
- Cross insurance.
- Continuation or contingency plan.
- Systems & procedures.

Goodwill

Most people do not take enough time and do not think logically about their options and end up 'marrying or selling to whoever's easy' or they have an inflated or unrealistic perception of value. Everyone thinks their firm is worth a trillion dollars. In most cases, people spend too much time thinking about the money and not thinking about the other issues, like how long will you stay?

Another stumbling block… the thinking that "I built this, I'm entitled to a return, and if you want access to my clients, you'll have to pay me dearly for it". The practice has to be cash flow affordable to the buyer but there also has to be a good enough book of business for the seller to earn anything on it.

A substantial obligation to previously retired partners or a repurchase obligation to other partners can be a big burden, too.
Some general considerations:

> • There is a value. I have come across many professional firms that do not recognise Goodwill for their own purposes but that doesn't mean that there is no Goodwill. Goodwill does exist and does have a value (providing of course we are talking about a good practice). It is in my view a most generous gesture to a future generation on the part of partners in a firm that ignore Goodwill

values today. Eventually the value will be realised – just as in any other business.

• A Sydney broker's experience. A broker in Sydney has recently in-formed me that he has been receiving around 20 inquiries per week from firms wishing to acquire other firms – they tend to be well run firms that are looking for expansion.

• Financial Planning – financial planning firms for some years have been selling on an average multiple of 3.3 times when accounting firms have been selling quite commonly for around 0.8 – 1.0 times. This raises the question – are they really worth more than accounting firms? Are accounting firms worth more?

• Any Goodwill calculations should be based on capitalisation of future maintainable earnings not on multiples of revenue as above.

• Profit is AFTER partners' commercial salaries and ROI. EBIT: most buyers are seeking 20% pa. Many firms don't achieve this… once allowance is made for commercial salaries and return on investment.

• The larger the practice – the harder to find a buyer.

What do you Want?

Succession planning is life planning. Ask yourself what you want to do for the rest of your life – what is the perfect scenario? Do you really want to retire completely or just begin taking more time off? Frame a plan that gets you as close as possible to your goals. Review the plan no less than once a year and never forget how quickly circumstances can change. If, for example, your retirement plans were based on the 2007 value of your investment portfolio, you might have to adjust drastically as a result of the 2008 global Financial Crisis. Depending on your investment strategy, your assets could have declined by as much as

40% to 60%. So you might have to work another two or more years to get to where you wanted to be - if your partners are amenable.

Criteria for Evaluating New Partners

Clear criteria for appointing a partner give firms a benchmark against which to evaluate candidates. For example, individuals being considered for future ownership in an accounting firm should have (most of these also apply to other professions):

• Completed a minimum of eight years of public accounting experience.

• Earned professional qualifications.

• Expressed interest in a specialization that meets the firm's needs.

• Set managerial goals and met them based on their expressed interest or specialization.

• Demonstrated ability to charge-and collect-an acceptable hourly billing rate (by market).

• Completed a series of professional development courses, from basic levels to executive management.

• Participated in practice development activities such as -

  ° Joining professional, civic or social organizations.

  ° Attending professional meetings.

  ° Holding office or directorship in civic, professional or alumni organizations.

  ° Speaking or making other professional appearances.

  ° Meeting with prospective clients and other business con-tacts.

  ° Developing new business from existing clients.

  ° Keeping clients informed on matters of importance to them.

• Displayed acceptable moral and ethical character.

• Demonstrated temperate health habits.

• Obtained the support of his or her spouse.

- Shown responsibility in personal financial affairs.
- Espoused personal goals that don't conflict with firm goals.
- Developed good interpersonal skills.
- Gained the respect of partners, staff and clients.

Criteria for Evaluating Ongoing Partners

- New client growth.
- Net recoverable fee growth.
- New services to existing and new clients.
- Higher hourly realization.
- Realizable hours and average dollar recovery attributable to the partner.
- Demonstrable improvement in technical competency.
- Improvement in quality of team members' skill set / productivity.
- Other contributions to the firm's capability.
- Client attrition / feedback
- Team member attrition / feedback
- True profitability- partner net profit recovered per hour.

Strategic Planning

Succession planning is life planning and any planning involves three basic questions - Now? Where? How? Where are we now; where do we want to be; and how are we going to get there. It is surprising how few professional firms have a process of strategic planning and if they do, fail to implement the strategies contained therein.

Succession is only one of many issues requiring attention in an average firm but it is fast becoming, if it has not already, the most critical issue.

Summary

If you are an accounting professional, in particular, like the planning you do for your clients, succession planning is an ongoing process. As your clients who are contemplating retirement cannot develop and implement a plan one year prior to transition and hope to fulfill their retirement dreams, neither can a professional practitioner. As our professions move forward and becomes more competitive, it is imperative to build transferable business value and create a plan to realise that value through business transition.

Once you've decided to retire, there's some risk that you'll lose interest in the job. Setting goals can help you stay interested and focused. Create an inventory of content knowledge. Plan to transmit knowledge about your position that will be critical to your successor, such as professional knowledge or historical knowledge about the firm. It's also important to create an inventory of process knowledge. You do many things instinctively. Now is the time to become more conscious of the processes you use, so you can pass them on to your successor. Seeking independent advice may speed up the process – objectives can be achieved a lot sooner.

CHAPTER SUMMARY

•   A generation of managing partners who founded their firms have already commenced to retire. The autocratic, entrepreneurial founder tends to stay longer, and the longer he/she stays, the less likely the firm is to survive to the next generation. You can cause your firm's stagnation and demise by staying too long because it's hard to give up that power.

•   Training of selected partners for leadership and practice management will take on more importance. Few firms presently provide training in these areas. Informal networks, however, are currently providing the opportunity for these young partners or partners elect to experience 'real life' issues and practical experiences.

•   Are you building a business or a book of business? A critical question.

•   Advisers need good advice too! Some critical issues to consider.

•   Goodwill…. Most people do not take enough time and do not think logically about their options and end up 'marrying or selling to whoever's easy' or they have an inflated or unrealistic perception of value. Everyone thinks their firm is worth a trillion dollars.

•   Criteria for evaluating new partners …Clear criteria for appointing a partner give firms a benchmark against which to evaluate candidates.

•   Criteria for evaluating ongoing partners.

CHAPTER 11
DOGS, CATS, RATS & PIGEONS!

(Or How to Value Goodwill in a Professional Firm)

In recent times the matter of valuing Goodwill in an accounting practice, in particular, has gained prominence and it seems to me that there is much said and written that borders on being pure nonsense! Change is overtaking this profession so rapidly that many of the more traditional views about Goodwill no longer have relevance. We accountants are very strong on technical skills and we like to work with set formulae and calculations but markets don't necessarily work that way and lately we have been witnessing a lot of activity in practice mergers, sales and listings that suggest that our methods of valuation are all over the place.

For longer than I care to remember the 'cents in the $' approach has been widely accepted often without reference to the real net profit and all too often without thorough due diligence (or any due diligence). I was astonished at one recent case where a bank took possession of a very badly managed practice, generating losses, to recover their debt. Receivers were appointed for this practice with over $500,000 fees. The practice was advertised for sale only twice that I am aware of. A client firm approached me for assistance. The sale had no claw back provision and in fact no ongoing involvement or support whatsoever from the vendors. All staff where of a very mature age (not necessarily a disadvantage) but ongoing involvement was limited. Information provided was sketchy. I suggested that my client should offer 30 cents in the $. However, what was effectively a 'list of fees' sold quickly for 80 cents in the $ I understand that 18 tenders were received! It was all over and done within a couple of weeks.

Clearly demand is exceeding supply at this time and feedback suggests that for every seller there are twelve potential buyers on average.

Consolidators

"Consolidators' remain active although working more discretely in the profession. In Australia WHK and others appear to have shown how this can be done successfully. In a little more than ten years WHK have moved from establishment to being the fifth largest accounting firm in Australia and has targeted an index rating in the ASX TOP 200. It reported a net profit of just under 9% for 2005/2006. It has built funds under management to around $7 billion and share price has almost doubled in less than 5 years. Each time I check they seem to have acquired yet another quality firm in either Australia or New Zealand. The market has looked upon all of this activity with much interest and banks, especially have been acquiring shares. Total market capitalization is now around 13-14 times profit or perhaps a more traditional way of viewing this might be to say $1.17 - $1.26 (by my calculation) in the $1 Count have commenced activity to build a new listed accounting firm and I am aware of many others. Many, many smaller acquisitions and mergers have been and continue to take place.

Yet in the midst of all of this I continue to read commentary from our 'expert' consultants in the professional journals and media generally that firms with turnover in excess of $2 million have no Goodwill value! One firm with over $10 mil turnover recently contacted me to advise that they were merging with another firm with around $4-5 mil and that firm had been independently valued by an 'expert' valuer at NIL! How can this be? I recognize that a valuation based upon a multiple of net earnings after allowing for commercial partners' salaries could realize that sort of result but surely an established firm with intellectual capital, branding, staff, processes and infrastructure has a value, especially in today's market? Economies of scale alone would suggest that there will be some gain overall. There will be need for much change and careful development of HR strategies but a well-managed new merged entity surely would benefit from this. Bearing in mind the difficulties in securing experienced, skilled staff in today's climate just this factor alone must have significant value.

The Last Man Standing

My understanding is that many large firms now ignore Goodwill in the balance sheets to make it easier to move partners in and out of these firms. As a policy decision that may have some merit in some situations but it doesn't remove the fact that Goodwill still exists. Even Price Waterhouse Coopers with its turnover of $1.25 billion has a value even though for internal purposes they decide to ignore Goodwill to make it easier to secure and release partners. As a former partner of Coopers & Lybrand it has often occurred to me that the 'last man standing' will be an incredibly wealthy person. Should this firm decide to list and I believe that this is inevitable in time a handful of equity partners at the end of the partnership will realize incredible wealth.

Superstition

I am reminded of the story of the superstitious pigeons in writing this book. B.F.Skinner was right: You can make a pigeon superstitious. Just put it in a cage and arrange for food to appear at regular intervals. Whatever the pigeon happens to be doing just as the food arrives – spinning around, bobbing its head, whatever- it will keep doing, over and over again, in the hope that the dance caused the food to appear.

The pigeon will assume a cause-and-effect relationship that doesn't really exist. That's what superstition is: a compulsion to take an action that has no actual influence on the desired outcome. Many sportsmen have been known to continue to wear their favourite football boots, shorts, undies or whatever well after their use by date because they did so well the first time they used that item of clothing.

Once we have made up our mind we are like the pigeons and these sportsmen. We don't want to change our behavior, regardless of how much data we see to support a new and better alternative. It's easier to be superstitious, easier to hope that the food will just slide out of the dispenser when we spin around and around. Accountants especially like set formulae and simple calculations. Times have changed dramatically though – we haven't experienced anything like this before; the 'baby boomer' phenomenon, demand in excess of supply, severe staff shortage, the strongest demand for our services that we have ever seen, rapidly changing and developing computer systems and so on. Intellectual capital is beginning to gain recognition, not just in our profession, but worldwide in any business, as the most valuable asset yet we will still write-off annually the full cost of labour without recognizing the improved value of the experience and skills to our business.

Our current circumstances may not last – five to ten years from now most baby boomers will have retired, technology will have moved on in leaps and bounds, the professions of today will hardly be recognizable then – and a whole new approach to valuation will be required again. Can we continue to justify our current 'superstitious' methods of valuation?

The Bobbing and Dancing Goes On!

My argument is that many firms are worth far more (and some far less) than independent valuations suggest. Greater due diligence is required with far more attention given to the value of intellectual capital, the knowledge base and infrastructure overall. How can a valuer seriously argue that a long-established firm with over $4 mil turnover, accumulated intellectual capital, a strong knowledge base and very good infrastructure has no value? The bobbing and dancing goes on! How is it that Financial Planning firms have a much higher value than accounting firms – is it any wonder that much of the interest in acquiring accounting firms is coming from Financial Planning groups? How did the accounting profession lose this service? How does one value audit fees in today's climate? New audit registrations are virtually impossible to secure for medium to small firms so that if there is no succession for registered auditors in a firm surely the audit fees have no ongoing value?

Some years ago I predicted a strong reduction in the number of firms in Australia and New Zealand through the acquisitions, mergers, consolidations and 'roll ups' that would take place. That prediction is being realized. We now have many more firms in the $3 mil turnover and over range and for many of these there is a deliberate strategy to secure the size and infrastructure that makes them more attractive to the likes of WHK. In my view WHK has an assured future. Many of the smaller firms are disappearing but there will always by a niche market for successful small firms providing very personal service. For these firms net profit (before partners' salaries) in the order of 50% - 60% is achievable. Many other firms will continue to spin on their wheels without moving forward – the 'tyre-kickers' of our profession who will not make any progressive decisions – the laggards of our profession..... waiting to see what happens as the world passes them by!

Perhaps it is time to re-visit the definition of "Goodwill" or perhaps even look more seriously at valuing other intangibles such as branding, intellectual capital, knowledge base and infrastructure. The biggest risk accountants would perceive in all of this is over-valuation. Over valuation due to Goodwill was one of the biggest factors of the dot.com bust. However, even looking at these factors with our most conservative glasses on should in my view still show value – not Nil as in the case mentioned above.

Dogs, Cats and Rats

A key measure is the strength of your "positive net influences", i.e. the strength of those clients who help "sell" your attributes in the workplace, community and business, and will they stick?

Legally defined Goodwill is "Nothing more than the probability that the old customers will revert to the old place even though the old trader has gone" (Lord Eldon in Crutwell v. Lye). But is it really that simple today? I do recall many years ago being involved in the valuation of a very successful hotel in a dispute between a lessee and the owner and my research found a case where the judge referred to Goodwill as being akin to dogs, cats & rats. The 'dogs' will always remain loyal to the master and will follow the master wherever he/she goes (in this instance an argument favouring the lessee); the cats will remain with the 'house' because it is convenient and they have always 'lived there' (favours the landlord); and finally the 'rats' ….well they will go where they get the best deal – food or in the case of our clients, price. I love this analogy and suspect that it really applies more to accounting firms than to hotels! I suspect that we should look a lot more closely at this analogy but then many contracts include provision for 'clawback' so if the clients such as the cats and rats don't stay the purchaser doesn't pay in any event. But none of this 'traditional' thinking on practice value considers the newly recognized intangibles such as branding, intellectual capital, infrastructure, knowledge base, copyright, etc. Many practices would be very surprised if they produced a list of tools, templates and intellectual property. I recently attempted this on my own business and found a list of 100 without really trying!

Ideally of course, the valuation of Goodwill should be based on the profits that the block of clients will generate rather than the additional gross fees they will produce. The aim of the purchaser should be to create profit rather than to merely acquire supplementary turnover. Going back, once again, to the case of the $4 mil firm that supposedly had a NIL value and particularly considering that this is a merger I would be looking at the potential to produce synergies in the new merged firm. A merger such as this creates the ideal opportunity as catalyst for change in both firms. Seasoned campaigners, who have gone through the process of purchasing a practice on more than one occasion, have identified the achievable synergies as a significant consideration in the overall deal.

The scope for increased productivity and reduced overheads can have a significant effect on the multiples used and the eventual valuation of the purchase price. As a minimum step a comprehensive five-way budget should be completed (contact me for a copy of the template). To my surprise this is often not done – with firms explaining that they have been simply too busy with too many client and other distractions! What would you advise your clients in this situation? A review of the potential synergies should include reviewing the increased expertise and specialism, reduction in staff numbers overall, reduction in office space overall, economic usage of equipment and software, reduction in general overheads and improved quality of service, ability to drill down into the 'fields of diamonds' (refer to previous paper by David Connell – contact me for a copy) such as financial services, succession planning, strategic planning and financial analysis. Recent surveys reveal that there are four vacancies for every accountant in Australian and New Zealand firms. Perhaps this alone could be one of the most compelling reasons for a practice acquisition or merger.

It was recently suggested to me that a firm that does not have a time recording system should be valued down. What about fixed pricing and value-pricing? Many firms have embraced this concept in recent times with some deliberately doing away with time sheets. A whole new area of argument and debate!

So much has been written about this subject of valuation of Goodwill for professional firms that it was not my intention to simply add to this and especially not to regurgitate traditional or 'superstitious' (as for the pigeons!) ideas. Rather I am attempting to generate some serious thinking as to whether our current approach is right. I'm particularly seeking feedback from readers.

CHAPTER SUMMARY

- In recent times the matter of valuing Goodwill in an accounting practice, in particular, has gained prominence and it seems to me that there is much said and written that borders on being pure nonsense!

- Once we have made up our mind we are like the pigeons. We don't want to change our behaviour, regardless of how much data we see to support a new and better alternative. It's easier to be superstitious, easier to hope that the food will just slide out of the dispenser when we spin around and around. Accountants especially like set formulae and simple calculations.

- Five to ten years from now most baby boomers will have retired, technology will have moved on in leaps and bounds, the professions of today will hardly be recognizable then – and a whole new approach to valuation will be required again. Can we continue to justify our current 'superstitious' methods of valuation?

- How is it that Financial Planning firms have a much higher value than accounting firms – is it any wonder that much of the interest in acquiring accounting firms is coming from Financial Planning groups?

- Dogs, cats and rats …an old court case that makes much sense.

CHAPTER 12
ETHICS – OLD FASHIONED OR INCONVENIENT?

Some years ago I was scheduled to speak at a major conference of one of the professional bodies and a few days before commencement I received a call from the manager and organizer who was in something of a panic state. A speaker scheduled to speak on ethics was a 'last minute' withdrawal. He asked if I would be willing to provide a presentation on this subject and I was very quick to say "Yes". Perhaps a little too quick! But I instantly recognized the importance of the topic and felt honoured that I should be approached to do this albeit in these circumstances. Subsequently, with a little research and reading, I realized what a difficult topic I had taken on. Many, more qualified persons than I have taken on this subject. Surfing the net I quickly realized that this is the realm of philosophers and saints. I suspect that, in part, I was chosen because of my (then) 36 years in the profession and the fact that 20 of those years were with the major firms – mostly as a partner, and today I am a consultant to practitioners. I could hardly be seen to be either philosopher or saint!

The presentation was a plenary session and so a good roll up ensued…I suspect for many, perhaps half heartedly at commencement! This chapter, in part, records the paper I presented that day. I had decided to provide only a relatively short session and open up the topic for discussion. I was told later that this session recorded the highest rating from attendees for the conference. The discussion was really quite amazing with some attendees who quite hot under the collar because of what they viewed as their personal adherence to the rules whilst, in their opinion, many of their competitors did not! I don't think I have ever witnessed elsewhere such heated discussion from a group of professionals.

It is my personal view that 'Ethics', as prescribed in most 'rules' of professional bodies are the bare minimum, mandatory standards required. These organizations spend many hours on researching the appropriate wording and over a great many years have a wealth of experience to draw upon. They also have to be cognizant of the voluminous statutory requirements impacting upon their members and the differing opinions in interpretation. The writings on the subject of ethics in professional bodies are endless. Accordingly I can only express my personal views on this important subject.

But let's start with a dictionary definition of the word 'ethics':
Ethics: science of morals, study of principles of human duty; treatise of this; moral principles; rules of conduct.
This is a very topical issue throughout the world through a number of events not the least of which are:

- The events of 11th September 2001.
- The developments in embryonic stem cell harvesting, cloning, etc.
- The Enron collapse in America.
- The HIH collapse in Australia.
- The demise of Andersons worldwide… one of the largest professional firms in the world at the time.
- The document-shredding scandal involving Clayton Utz
- The Merrill's stockbrokers' saga.
- The 2008 global financial crisis that many would argue was the

result of greed and lack of ethics on a world-wide scale.

- The many, many political scandals...where does one begin? ...
  how long is a piece of string?
- As I write this News Corp is making headline news in the UK and
  elsewhere for all of the wrong reasons.

... to name just a few that come to my mind!

Two key issues to emerge through all of this are that:

- Many professionals have lost their high standing for
  trustworthiness.
- Regulation does not force people to act in the public interest.

As one of the "baby boomer' generation in today's society I have come
through the years when there has been a very strong emphasis on
the so called 'work ethic' wherein I and many of my peers have firmly
believed that it is necessary to work very hard and to 'put in the hours'
to grow a business or to earn a living. I suspect that history will record
our generation as the generation that worked harder not smarter. Today
I see evidence of this in virtually every practice I go into – practitioners
working long hours to the detriment of their own health, their family, their
own personal growth, their personal philosophy or values (and this is
where the stress comes into play); social involvement; and all too often
their own wealth!

Life Balance - Lifestyle

My observations reveal that Generation 'X' and Generation 'Y' have
a very different view of life. "Life balance" is their catch cry. More
particularly "Lifestyle" – they are not going to work as hard: they have
already shown that they are anxious to work smarter. They will take full
advantage of technology, especially the Internet, which is still only in

its infancy. It is plain to me that this new generation has its goal firmly focused on values that my generation finds hard to relate to. The work ethic being one of the more obvious. Daily we read articles now in the press about attempts by large corporations to address this and the new emphasis on 'Culture'. These journalists explain that family is taking on a new importance and this new generation simply will not be prepared to let their career or occupation interfere with their relationships. Whilst money is no longer the driving force the reality is that Generation 'X' and Generation 'Y' will earn more than the 'Baby Boomers' have ever dreamed of – and they will do it smarter not harder!

I'm afraid I remain sceptical about all of this and have yet to see the evidence that convinces me that family values are improving, that relationships are stronger and longer-lasting and that workers have more time for relaxation. I have recently read that in Australia over 80% of mothers now work in outside employment …whether they want to or not! Marriages have difficulty surviving, even in the short term because of lack of commitment and selfishness. I hope I'm wrong but there seems to be a growth in the culture of hedonistic materialism rather than any real improvement in values and ethics.

Never have we expected more of leadership – and never have we been so disappointed. Leaders do find it tough to ensure that their people adhere to values and ethics. The prevailing principles in business lead to employees asking, "What's in it for me?" Missing are those that would make them think, "What's good, right, and just for everyone?" A great many executives believe the purpose of business is business itself and greed is good so long as the authorities don't find out. There is a huge gulf between theory and practice of ethics. "Do as I say; not as I do" is the guiding motto of many leaders. Hit by fraud, deceit, and greed, people are angry about the lack of values and ethics in business. It is time for business leaders to ask if decisions are good for society as well as for their own businesses; leaders must serve a higher purpose (refer to earlier comments throughout this book and, in particular, quotes from Viktor Frankl).

High Moral Purpose

Businesses often behave as though they're willing to do anything to survive, even if that means destroying the world in which they operate. They would do better to pursue the common good – not because it is right or fashionable but to ensure their sustainability. No business or profession will survive over the long run if it doesn't offer value to customers or clients, create a future that rivals cannot, and maintain the common good. Wise leaders set their sights high and have a moral purpose. In the relentless pursuit of excellence they demand the highest level of ethics in their business and work.

Our lives will never be quite the same after 11th September 2001. The threshold of our vulnerability has been raised forever. Entering a museum, crossing a bridge, or flying in a plane will not be quite the same experience as pre September 11th. We have lost certain innocence. What looms before us is an unknown future. Trouble spots appear across the globe – any of which could change our lives overnight. All of us have had to experience the extra security precautions taken at our airports: taking computers out of bags; batteries out of computers; removing steel capped shoes or heavy boots; and so on.
I am concerned for my children and grandchildren. Surely how we respond now will make a difference.

Surely the answer to the title of this chapter is a very loud, resounding

"NO". Now more than ever we must seriously address this issue of ethics. Let's be honest up front though – you cannot legislate for good behavior, good ethics or moral character. Professional practitioners themselves must possess certain individual virtues if they are to be truly ethical. Merely following the rules will not be enough. Ultimately it is a professional's own personal virtue which will enable them to act ethically. Our professional bodies attempt to lay down the foundations in which to guide ethical behavior but I believe strongly that it really is the individual who is accountable. We should not be looking to our professional bodies to act as policemen and any standards which they set can really be only the bare minimum.

Values

We hear a lot about 'values' in business today and society is placing in-creasing demands on business to improve values. Quite often perhaps it is hypocritical but the fact remains that society expects much more of business leaders today. The turnover of CEO's has never been higher because short-termism rules! Markets, media, government and analysts all focus on today rather than building for tomorrow. Society is demanding that corporations act with good governance – recent failures have placed pressure upon politicians to legislate to improve this. But it really comes down to leaders 'walking the talk'. The reality at present is that there is a very real narcissistic culture or value held by many CEO's and leaders of businesses and professional practices. They fail to understand that an individual is only ever as successful as the shoulders of the people that they stand on. Too many believe that they have the personal attributes on their own to achieve success. Eventually – sooner or later – their weaknesses are exposed and hence the increasing turnover of CEO's and leaders of businesses.

A Choice has to be Made

I find it quite disturbing that so few professional firms have even attempted to determine what the values of their individual firms are let alone 'walk the talk'. The larger the firm the more important this becomes. Stress comes when an individual is working with an organization where his or her personal values are in conflict with that of the organization that he or she works with. It is often very simple things.

For example have you ever come across these scenarios?:

1. A firm espouses honesty in all its dealings. A phone call comes into a receptionist from a client to speak to a partner. The receptionist calls the partner advising: "Joe Blow wishes to speak to you urgently". The partner responds: "Tell Joe I'm not in!" A simple example but the partner is clearly not walking the talk and the message sent to the employee, the receptionist, is that it is OK to lie sometimes! Values are immediately compromised.

2. An "A" client phones your receptionist and when unable to reach you, uses a string of 'expletive deletives'. Your receptionist explains to you that she shouldn't have to put up with this. How do you act?

3. The most serious of course is the client that makes it clear to you that you are to act against the law, the community interests or your own values in representing him/her.

Ultimately, a choice has to be made. This choice involves choosing between an ethical decision and an unethical decision. The virtues, which I consider are essential to warranting ethical behaviour, are:

• Honesty & integrity
• Trustworthiness and faithfulness.
• Reliability and dependability.

• Ability to care about others.

If you want people to think you "care", you actually have to care!

You can't do it with 'tick box' cliques, donations and tokenism.

There are two major barriers:

• Lack of education and training.

• Failure to distinguish between ethics and law.

As professionals we must act virtuous if our profession is to be moral. We must balance both our professional responsibilities to our employees and clients, but also our obligation to represent and protect the public interest and this is where today's headlines are showing up our weakness. Too many professionals seem prepared to place themselves in a position of virtually being executives of their clients and acting in their client's best interests to the detriment of the community.

Professionals who act in a trusted manner can be considered to be ethical not because they are following the rules but because they would do what is right anyway, regardless of the means or situation. Ethical professionals can be relied upon to perform their tasks promptly and in a manner required by their clients or employers. Concern for others and a continual concern as to what they do as professionals allows a professional to honour public trust.

I am a firm believer that the vast majority of professionals do act ethically in their dealings. It is a minority that bring our professions into disrepute. The important thing is that your clients, your staff and your community already know whether you 'walk the talk'. Their judgment has already been made. There is, however, always room for improvement – perhaps now is the time for you personally to consider whether you are 'walking the talk'.

Philosophy

Earlier in this chapter and elsewhere in this book I mentioned "life balance". There are many books today that address this issue and it is important that you take time out to consider where you rank in this. Your philosophy or values is an important part of this balance of life. If you haven't given adequate consideration to this in the past then now is the time to do so. I mentioned at the outset that this book would reflect my personal views. My own ethic is a Christian ethic – Catholic to be more precise- and my philosophy is based upon the Ten Commandments and the teachings of Jesus Christ and the Catholic Church. I respect your rights to your faith or beliefs whatever they may be but at the end of the day I suspect that all of us share the desire to build a better world.

To do so we must agree on certain minimum standards and rules. These are the signposts of life – without rules for example how would we control traffic? The rules of the road are there for the benefit of all: In Australia, drive on the left side of the road; give way to the right; and so on. Imagine the chaos if we didn't have these rules! People do break these rules and often pay the penalty accordingly. As already stated we cannot legislate for good behaviour, good ethics or moral character. Whatever the law, individuals will still make choices for better or worse!

Knowledge Now Has a Premium

Human Resources is a new growth profession but most practitioners haven't yet woken up to the enormous benefit that these professionals can provide to our practices. Since 1914 the value of commodities around the world has declined in value by a staggering 84%. During this same period the value of intellectual capital has simply soared. How else can we explain the values the market gives to our larger companies on the Stock Exchange? The Commonwealth Bank in Australia, for example, is valued at many times the net value of its tangible assets. Quite clearly markets around the world are placing stronger value on people. Tangible assets depreciate in value. People, with their skills and experience, increase in value and the world is now coming to grips with this realization. Knowledge now has a premium. Why then wouldn't you invest in increasing this value through training and culture development? In my profession, accountants have been dreadfully slow in coming to this understanding but some, still very much in a minority, are now investing in human resources strategies and reaping the rewards. Our profession overall, in at least some quarters, is still seen to be 'employer of last resort'. We won't become employers of 'first choice' until we make our profession a lot more attractive to young people. And that involves addressing with much greater focus and determination the issue of proper culture development, identifying clearly for all stakeholders, our values and walking the talk. Understand that money is not the driving force for Generation 'X' or Generation 'Y', lifestyle, relationships and values are. If your practice hasn't considered culture development, values and ethics as an important strategy for the growth and survival of your practice then you are not even in the race. To consider ethics as old-fashioned or inconvenient is to write the death warrant for your own business or profession. If you're having trouble securing good people now have a good hard look at your practice and consider what the real reason might be!

Sir Charles Court put all of this succinctly in an article when he said: "It is crucial to remember that although an ethical stand might result in a short-term dollar loss, experience teaches us that it soon brings rewards beyond measure". Overall our professions must actively seek to instruct its members on the long-term value of ethical behaviour.

The primary Christian value is stated in the golden rule:

"So whatever you wish that men would do to you, do so to them".

CHAPTER SUMMARY

• 'Ethics', as prescribed in most 'rules' of professional bodies are the bare minimum, mandatory standards required. These organizations spend many hours on researching the appropriate wording and over a great many years have a wealth of experience to draw upon. They also have to be cognizant of the voluminous statutory requirements impacting upon their members and the differing opinions in interpretation. The writings on the subject of ethics in professional bodies are endless.

• Never have we expected more of leadership – and never have we been so disappointed. Leaders do find it tough to ensure that their people adhere to values and ethics. The prevailing principles in business lead to employees asking, "What's in it for me?" Missing are those that would make them think, "What's good, right, and just for everyone?"

• No business or profession will survive over the long run if it doesn't offer value to customers or clients, create a future that rivals cannot, and maintain the common good. Wise leaders set their sights high and have a moral purpose.

• Our professional bodies attempt to lay down the foundations in which to guide ethical behaviour but I believe strongly that it's really is the individual who is accountable. We should not be looking to our professional bodies to act as policemen and any standards which they set can really be only the bare minimum.

• My observations reveal that Generation 'X' and Generation 'Y' have a very different view of life. "Life balance" is their catch cry. More particularly "Lifestyle" – they are not going to work as hard: they have already shown that they are anxious to work smarter. It is plain to me that this new generation has its goal firmly focused on values that my generation finds hard to relate to. The work ethic being one of the more obvious.

- Surely the answer to the title of this chapter is a very loud, resounding "NO". You cannot legislate for good behaviour, good ethics or moral character. Professional practitioners themselves must possess certain individual virtues if they are to be truly ethical. Merely following the rules will not be enough. Ultimately it is a professional's own personal virtue which will enable them to act ethically.

- I find it quite disturbing that so few professional firms have even attempted to determine what the values of their individual firms are let alone 'walk the talk'. The larger the firm the more important this becomes.

- If you want people to think you "care", you actually have to care! You can't do it with 'tick box' cliques, donations and tokenism.

- Quite clearly markets around the world are placing stronger value on people. Tangible assets depreciate in value. People, with their skills and experience, increase in value and the world is now coming to grips with this realization. Knowledge now has a premium. Why then wouldn't you invest in increasing this value through training and culture development?

- Our profession overall, in at least some quarters, is still seen to be 'employer of last resort'. We won't become employers of 'first choice' until we make our profession a lot more attractive to young people.

CHAPTER 13
THE BOILING FROG

Many readers will be familiar with the story of the boiling frog. An old story but very relevant to today's professional practitioners. Its message is that a frog can be boiled alive if the water is heated slowly enough—it is said that if a frog is placed in boiling water, it will jump out, but if it is placed in cold water that is slowly heated, it will continue trying to adapt and never jump out and will eventually boil alive!

The story is generally told in a figurative context, with the upshot being that people should make themselves aware of gradual change lest they suffer a catastrophic loss. Often it is used to illustrate a slippery slope argument. For example even minor increases in government legislation say in tax, by making them seem less noteworthy, make future increases in that legislation more likely: What would once have seemed a huge tax change, the argument goes, now becomes seen as just another incremental increase, and thus appears more palatable. In the boiling-frog allegory, the frog represents the average professional firm, whilst the gradual heating of the water represents the incremental changes that are building up in our professions to a "Tsunami" of change.

At a time when professional firms should be striving for greater success—in line with the rest of the world—many have become the last bastion of resistance to change. The first step to change is to recognize the barriers holding us back and work through them.
What then are the barriers preventing us from achieving greater success?

Complacency

Profits generally are good—if you can't make a good profit in your chosen profession then you shouldn't be in practice. Government legislation changes in the last 10 –20 years have been quiet overwhelming and our professions have done an outstanding job in coping with this on behalf of our clients. Our clients have never needed us more. The demand far exceeds the supply. And yet amidst all of this we are overlooking huge opportunities and in many instances we have ceased to provide true value services to our clients because of the oversupply of work. The vast bulk of our activity for many professions is now in compliance work and we have relinquished the quality value work to specialists. There appears to be a lack of imagination – if I can't imagine a better way or a better world then I'm not likely to achieve it. Again this goes back to our VISION.

Strategic Planning and Goal Setting

Very few firms have processes in place to seriously consider strategies and future directions. Most are distracted on a daily basis by operational issues and client distractions & demands. And even those who do attempt to look at strategies try do so in a rushed annual 'retreat' without any clear understanding as to what is happening in the wider profession and so have a very limited inward looking approach to the review. Some utilize independent chairpersons or facilitators who have no understanding or experience in their profession.

Lack of Resources Applied

 New projects, assignments or tasks affecting the firm are approached without serious effort or resources. All too often personnel are requested to undertake any efforts in their own time. Whilst our intention is genuinely to meet with success our overall effort invested does little to ensure success. There is a big difference between a "chance of success" and a "leave nothing to chance" approach.

Lack of Commitment

There is a huge difference between commitment and support. It is not uncommon to find all partners/ directors in agreement on an issue in the boardroom and espousing full support but as soon as they leave the boardroom the commitment has gone. Commitment means doing everything possible to bring about success in a particular task.

Lack of accountability

Tasks are often set and goals made without a system of accountability or timelines. The highest form of accountability is self– accountability. In world-class organizations it is the willingness of personnel to be accountable that sets them apart from other organizations.

Procrastination

Quite often leaders in a firm are fully aware of the changes that they need to make but days, weeks and years flow by without the necessary action being taken. More often than not some external impetus is required to get action under way usually involving an independent facilitator.

First amongst equals

Lack of a specific leader who determines the strategic direction of the firm and is accountable for results can be very difficult to achieve in a partnership—who is first amongst equals! Without consensus it just doesn't happen and everyone tries to contribute to leadership with resultant inefficiencies.

Lack of Effort

The difference between the maximum amount of effort an employee can bring to his/her position and the actual effort he/she is currently producing is sometimes referred to as the 'effort gap'. By meeting the minimum requirement the employee has already done what is necessary to avoid penalty—any effort after this is discretionary.

Lack of Vision

The very successful book "Built to Last" refers to clear vision as one of the major success factors and refers to a "BHAG" or Big Hairy Audacious Goal—something everyone can grab hold of and own. Improving net profit, doubling fees and the like are not BHAG's. What will the firm actually look like in 5 years' time? Staff wants to know. It is not unusual for staff to leave a firm through dissatisfaction with the lack of leadership, management and vision—only to find the firm they go to is much the same!

Lack of Concentration

On average employees are interrupted every 10 minutes during our workday… phones, emails, interruptions by others. These interruptions hinder our ability to do our best work. Time management is a skill that firms generally do not give due recognition to. I came across a firm that utilizes miniature red traffic cones—personnel place one of these next to their desk if they do not want to be interrupted because of work pressures—simple but very effective! A cone of silence!

Culture/HR

In recent times this has taken on greater importance than ever but strangely I still hear professionals ask "What is HR?". Understanding what makes your people tick is now more important than ever—staff recruitment and retention are now vital. Again however, very few firms have either part-time or full-time resources in this area or if they do, do not give these professionals sufficient scope to apply strategy. Many simply focus on Occupational Health & Safety or compliance activity.

Cost v Value.

In my profession of accounting we are highly trained technicians when it comes to knowing the cost of something and our clients pay us well for good advice in this area, however, the trap we often fall into is that we become just like our clients and look to the cost without considering the value in our own business. The cost of a job flow monitoring software package for example may seem high upon initial examination but the efficiencies to be gained over time may far, far outweigh that initial cost. All too often though firms seek a 'magic bullet' with instant results and fail to consider the long term value. Over time these firms fall further and further behind in the marketplace or will eventually go down the same path as the boiled frog. On the other side of the coin we frequently fail to see or explain the value we provide to clients and sell 6 minute units of time as our main revenue source.

Of course there are many other barriers but these twelve barriers sum up the main obstacles to growth and success in our firms. All can be over-come with focus and action plans. Quite often 'outside' assistance is needed, particularly where partners are not always in agreement as to who is the real leader.

The practice of the future will be very different from the practice of today. Some firms—the innovators & early adopters, are already moving very strongly to a new 'model' but most are still locked into yesterday's thinking. For example, again using the accounting profession as an example, it is generally considered acceptable to have a partner to staff ratio of around 7 or 8: 1 but there are already many firms working on ratios of 30-40:1. Many firms are now moving away from the concept of selling 6 minute units to value billing. Some firms experience far less difficulty in recruiting and retaining staff because they have outstanding 'employer of first choice' strategies.

Perhaps none of this discussion appeals to you and you are quite content—how warm is the water?

CHAPTER SUMMARY

- We are overlooking huge opportunities and in many instances we have ceased to provide true value services to our clients because of the oversupply of work. The vast bulk of our activity for many professions is now in compliance work and we have relinquished the quality value work to specialists.

- Very few firms have processes in place to seriously consider strategies and future directions. Most are distracted on a daily basis by operational issues and client distractions & demands.

- It is not uncommon to find all partners/ directors in agreement on an issue in the boardroom and espousing full support but as soon as they leave the boardroom the commitment has gone. Commitment means doing everything possible to bring about success in a particular task.

- Tasks are often set and goals made without a system of accountability or timelines. The highest form of accountability is self– accountability. In world-class organizations it is the willingness of personnel to be accountable that sets them apart from other organizations.

- Understanding what makes your people tick is now more important than ever—staff recruitment and retention are now vital.

- All too often though firms seek a 'magic bullet' with instant results and fail to consider the long term value. Over time these firms fall further and further behind in the marketplace or will eventually go down the same path as the boiled frog.

CHAPTER 14
BUILDING COMMITMENT: YOUR PEOPLE

Every professional practice should have a head; it should also have a heart. The size of that heart depends upon the size of employee commitment to its ideals and goals. If the partners/directors have very hazy ideals and goals then staff commitment will also be hazy or non-existent. Vitality in a practice has to be from the bottom up and must be developed. In the first chapter in this book I referred to Viktor Frankl's quote: "No man can tell another what his purpose is. Each must find out for himself, and must accept the responsibility that his answer prescribes" and if we read this in conjunction with Vince Lombardi: "The quality of a person's life is in direct proportion to their commitment to excellence, regardless of their field of endeavour" we begin to obtain some inkling that to achieve commitment and therefore success in our practice we must ensure that our people are attuned to and in full agreement with us. There must be a desire by each person to make it happen.

Do not underestimate how difficult it is to secure this desire or commitment. Employee commitment is a largely neglected realm of management, especially in professional firms, and within it lays a key to success for our professional practices in this rapidly changing world. The evidence is clear and I refer you again to the chapter in this book on leadership and in particular the following which I believe well worth repeating here –

Research has found that engaging your employees has never been more important than in the current environment of skills shortages and global war for talent. Highly engaged employees outperform disengaged counterparts by up to 28%. The improvement on your bottom line can be up to 57% greater. And then you have the additional challenges of high staff turnover and costs of recruitment where you have disengaged staff. Again Research (from the Mercer Survey of Australia at Work) shows nearly 25 per cent of Australian employees will change jobs this year. And when you consider staff turnover costs are up to 150 per cent of a person's annual salary it's obvious why staff retention is quickly becoming a burning management priority. The figures from the Mercer survey are valid, but some experts argue that they are only the tip of the iceberg. Professional firms need to factor in the costs of decreased productivity, lost investment in training and development, loss of revenue for key sales or management executives, administration set up, equipment purchase, recruitment costs, the new employee's induction into the firm's culture, management downtime in interviewing candidates, legal fees and payout commitments. There can be a lot more to staff turnover costs than first meets the eye, which is why it's so important to recruit the right candidate first off and then do what you can to keep them challenged, satisfied and engaged. When all of this is taken into account one begins to understand the true value of a good leader to a professional practice. Effective communication starts at the top.

Priorities

Over a period of many years now survey results show evidence of trends for increasing results of workplace stress, an increasing percentage of workers who are thinking seriously about quitting their jobs and other measures that are a serious indictment on employers. Further research has revealed that little personal control on the job was the single largest cause of burnout. Over many years I have facilitated many life balance workshops mostly for accounting practitioners but also other professionals. When the question is asked, "What do you consider to be the most important areas or roles in your life?" invariably "family" is the immediate response but when you examine more closely where time is spent again, invariably, the evidence is clearly in the area or role of work and career and this is the reason for so much stress in the workplace. We instinctively know where our priority should be but in practice we do the opposite!

Pressure in the workplace affects all of us in our lives and also has a substantial effect on productivity in our firms. I do frequently come across principals/ partners of professional firms who actually enjoy the cut and thrust of their daily lives, obviously love their work and work incredibly long hours. One person, in particular, that I recall was effectively the managing partner (no one ever disagreed with him so unofficially it was assumed that he was the 'managing partner' / the boss!) of a six-partner firm. He worked very long hours including weekends and was the undisputed outstanding performer in the practice – always exceeding other partners in productivity, fees rendered and so on. His health seemed fine. I was however aware that at home he had a wife and six children (so he must have spent some time at home!) and I have often wondered about the long-term effect on his wife and each of his children.

Our children are only with us for a relatively short time (my wife and I have five adult children) before they head off into that wide world to do their own thing and if we miss that opportunity for relationship building whilst they are at home it can never be recovered.
Most of our staff however see little merit in working harder and a principal reason given for their lack of enthusiasm for higher productivity

is the lack of incentive to work harder. One principal of a practice with over 30 staff has complained to me that if you stand in the hallway of his offices at 5.00 pm on Friday you could easily be killed in the stampede!

It is often claimed that fellow workers get the same pay increases and rewards regardless of how hard they work. I suspect however that whilst these claims are true the lack of drive has more to do with Viktor Frankl's assessment that no man can tell another what his purpose is. Each must find out for himself, and must accept the responsibility that his answer prescribes. Within ourselves we must ascertain our purpose. Earlier in this book I referred to the workers in a construction site and their varying attitudes from 'breaking rocks' to 'building a cathedral'. If all of our people are 'rock breakers' then it isn't too difficult to understand why they see little merit in working harder. But if we can foster an understanding of the bigger picture such as 'building a cathedral' and involve them in our mission or purpose so that there is a sharing of that purpose then I believe we are well on the way to building a hugely successful professional practice.

One of the major challenges for us is that workers don't see any link between their pay and their performance and they're out of the loop in communications, in involvement and in sharing success. Most do not believe that workers are a major beneficiary when productivity improves. If principals/partners are living in large homes, driving fancy cars and taking overseas trips how can they be convinced that they share in this success?

My Own Experience

My own experience in talking to staff of professional firms is that they do actually want to make a contribution. Staff want to have pride in their work and the practice they work for. If that is missing it simply becomes a work-to-rule job and motivation is quickly lost. I have mentioned previously that for many years I facilitated "Young Guns" meetings for up and coming young accountants and they made it very clear to me that they want to be noticed in positive ways, they want to be appreciated and they especially want to hear the two words 'thank you' when they do something well.

Generally speaking too, a firm's indifference to staff satisfaction and quality issues will be vividly on public display. In addition to speaking to the receptionist one only has to walk through an office to see whether there is pride in appearance, presentation and office layout. If you are not making the effort to instill pride in your workers the quality of your service will also suffer and it is quite apparent just how obvious this can become when one simply observes the behaviour of the 'director of first impressions', i.e. your receptionist. Over a period of many years I made it a habit to chat to the receptionist (all too often I was kept waiting in any event!) and the first question I would ask is "Do you know and understand your firm's mission?" In the majority of cases the blank look said it all (they may well have been thinking ... "this guy is a nutcase!"). Another question was: "Do you enjoy working here?" You would be amazed just how honest many people can be when this question is put to them and in most cases their employer would be shocked.

Here are some comments I have encountered:
- *"Most of us don't like working here but we have to work somewhere don't we?"*
- *"I want to do a good job. I really do. But no one appreciates it when we make the effort"*
- *"Ask my opinion? You're kidding? No one would ever listen to*

me."

• *"No one really cares – we just do our thing."*

• *"We are constantly told we have to reduce costs and we keep going without important equipment, training and help."*

• *"We all get paid to do a job. We are all important one way or another and staff are mostly good friends but when the results are good we don't see any improvement other than perhaps the partner's new car."*

• *"Mission? What's that?"*

• *"Business statement? No idea. We do tax I suppose."*

Involve Staff

I quite like a quote from Bill Creech, author of the Five Pillars of TQM, "If you will put the business in their hearts, they will put their hearts in the business". Some very clever people over the years have been working on this challenge and there is now much written as to suggestions and recommendations. Earlier in this book I have referred to Balanced Scorecard. I very much like the Balanced Scorecard approach to accountability and management as well as a positive way to involve staff and secure commitment and I highly recommend the use of this process. A recent Google of the words 'Balanced Scorecard' produced 2.1 million hits and you will find a wealth of information from the internet to assist you. Tailoring and simplification of the process is required for professional firms and I have found that it can be relatively simple to implement. Start with partners/principals and work with these in the first year to ensure that it is fully understood and any bugs removed before implementing with teams. The Balanced Scorecard must be synchronized with your Business Plan and strategies so ensure that your firm goals are very clear before embarking upon this path.

This approach to strategic management was first detailed in a series of articles and books by Drs. Kaplan and Norton. Recognizing some of the weaknesses and vagueness of previous management approaches, the Balanced Scorecard approach provides a clear prescription as to what companies should measure in order to 'balance' the financial perspective. The Balanced Scorecard is a management system (not only a measurement system) that enables organisations to clarify their vision and strategy and translate them into action. It provides feedback around both the internal business processes and external outcomes in order to continuously improve strategic performance and results. When fully deployed, the balanced scorecard transforms strategic planning from an academic exercise into the nerve centre of an enterprise.

The Balanced Scorecard suggests that we view the organization from four perspectives, and to develop metrics, collect data and analyse it relative to each of these perspectives:

The Learning & Growth Perspective

This perspective includes employee training and corporate cultural attitudes related to both individual and corporate self-improvement. In a knowledge-worker organization, people -- the only repository of knowledge -- are the main resource. In the current climate of rapid technological change, it is becoming necessary for knowledge workers to be in a continuous learning mode. Metrics can be put into place to guide managers in focusing training funds where they can help the most. In any case, learning and growth constitute the essential foundation for success of any knowledge-worker organization.

Kaplan and Norton emphasize that 'learning' is more than 'training'; it also includes things like mentors and tutors within the organization, as well as that ease of communication among workers that allows them to readily get help on a problem when it is needed.

The Business Process Perspective

This perspective refers to internal business processes. Metrics based on this perspective allow the managers to know how well their business is running, and whether its products and services conform to customer requirements (the mission). These metrics have to be carefully designed by those who know these processes most intimately; with our unique missions these are not something that can be developed by outside consultants.

The Customer (or client) Perspective

Recent management philosophy has shown an increasing realization of the importance of customer focus and customer satisfaction in any business. These are leading indicators: if customers are not satisfied, they will eventually find other suppliers that will meet their needs. Poor performance from this perspective is thus a leading indicator of future decline, even though the current financial picture may look good.

In developing metrics for satisfaction, clients should be analysed in terms of kinds of clients and the kinds of processes for which we are providing a service to those client groups.

The Financial Perspective

Kaplan and Norton do not disregard the traditional need for financial data. Timely and accurate funding data will always be a priority, and managers will do whatever necessary to provide it. In fact, often there is more than enough handling and processing of financial data. With the implementation of a corporate database, it is hoped that more of the processing can be centralized and automated. But the point is that the current emphasis on financials leads to the "unbalanced" situation with regard to other perspectives. There is perhaps a need to include additional financial-related data, such as risk assessment and cost-benefit data, in this category.

Time, cost and other resources are always limited in a professional practice but to ignore implementation of a process such is this one is to ignore the immense value that can be secured especially in commitment of our people. They become directly involved in the overall strategies of our Business Plan and individually involved through the specific linking of goals and objectives of the firm overall with their own personal purpose (Viktor Frankl again!). They become very directly involved in tailoring their own career path to grow with the firm.

The size of your firm will dictate the extent of your planning in this area but it is possible even for the smallest of firms to take on board the Balanced Scorecard concept. Unfortunately I have found all too often a resistance by professionals to become involved in this process often without even considering what the process is about and insisting that it is 'too difficult'. I have not found many professional firms utilizing this outstanding process but those that do have achieved marvellous results. I cannot think of any valid reasons for not embarking upon the process. Perhaps my recommendation that partners should be the starting point is a barrier that reduces their enthusiasm! And that leaves me to wondering whether there is some truth in a recent article published in the Australian Financial Review (24/5/11) under the heading "How to Get Along With a Narcissist and Survive". The article quotes extensively from psychotherapist and corporate coach Malcolm Dunn and his book, "Behind the Mask", and makes some astonishing if not controversial claims. In his earlier life Dunn admits to being a partner in consulting firms such as Accenture and Bain & Company and makes the following claim:

"In many cases, bad-tempered, bullying, self-indulgent behaviour is what you see among partners of professional services firms. One hundred per cent of those people have narcissistic behaviours."

Wow! What a statement to make! From my own experience I cannot agree with him but perhaps he is suggesting *…in varying degrees?* Of course he did not add this but as I read through his 'defining features' I began to think that perhaps even I had some narcissistic features. His definitions were very broad indeed and many of these were what I would consider to be normal business. Perhaps all of us need some serious self-examination from time to time to consider improvement. He uses some rather extreme examples such as the executive who boasted: "Every day I walk into the office, I can make the lives of 10,000 people completely miserable by doing very little". Perhaps the 'doing very little' is the key here.

If we don't bother to consider the use of processes such as Balanced Scorecard could we be considered to be 'doing very little' and therefore being narcissistic?

Meaningful Work

In this area of securing commitment there is no doubt that ideas come and go. I have seen so many variations for bonus arrangements over the years but so few of them actually work that I have become a sceptic of any proposals put to me for payment of bonuses and many of the surveys in recent years seem to be confirming that money is not the prime motivator for our people. We can be encouraged however by the great work being carried out by many professional researchers and if you really want to keep up to date with what is happening in the world of management and leadership I could recommend no better reading material than the monthly journal, Harvard Business Review. I read this journal every month from cover to cover and gain enormous value from the ideas contained therein. The issue of May 2011 is no exception with all articles in this issue worth a good read by professional practitioners and it contains an article specific to the topic of this chapter titled "The Power of Small Wins". An outstanding article, it confirms much of what I have written in this chapter.

I quote especially, "Through exhaustive analysis of diaries kept by knowledge workers, we discovered the progress principle: of all things that can boost emotions, motivation, and perceptions during a workday, the single most important is making progress in meaningful work". I am reminded of the firm with 60 staff that requested me to interview all of their staff and provide a report as to recommendations arising from this exercise. One young lady, in particular, made a huge impression upon me. She was qualified as an accountant, had excellent credentials and at age 28 had built very solid credentials and experience. To each staff member I had put a series of questions one of which was, "What do you consider to be the most important thing in your daily work?" To my astonishment and pleasant surprise she answered, "To walk out the front door at the end of each day feeling as though I have achieved something in my day". I further enquired, "Does that happen very often?" Her answer, "Very rarely if at all." I knew the partners had much admiration for this young lady and her work and when I later explained this to them they agreed that they would 'lift their own game' but unfortunately it was no real surprise to me to find out that within six months she had left this firm looking for challenge elsewhere.

The power of progress is fundamental to human nature. 'Crushing rocks' all day, every day can become incredibly tedious and unrewarding. In professional firms we have people who want to be creative. A further quote from the HBR article:

> *"In a dramatic rebuttal to the commonplace claim that high pressure and fear spur achievement, we found that, at least in the realm of knowledge work, people are more creative and productive when their inner work lives are positive – when they feel happy, are intrinsically motivated by the work itself, and have positive perceptions of their colleagues and the organization. Moreover, in those positive states, people are committed to the work and more collegial toward those around them."*

The research revealed that a 'best day' was any progress in the work by the individual or the team. Sad to say I couldn't count the number of times I have seen assignments delayed endlessly by partners who have work piled up behind them and effectively delay this process and the opportunity for staff to feel achievement and completion of a task. Like the young lady I mentioned above, if a person is motivated and happy at the end of a work day, it's a good bet that he or she made some progress. If the person drags out of the office disengaged and joyless, a setback is most likely to blame. Even small wins can boost inner work life tremendously. The work must be meaningful to the person doing it. I have encountered many professional practices where the work is very meaningful to principals/partners but staff carrying out the assignment simply has no appreciation of the value to the client and all too often have a completely wrong perspective of the value of the work they do. In one firm a sign was noticed stuck on the wall of a work station that read:

> *"Doing a good job here is like wetting your pants in a dark suit. You get a warm feeling, but no one else notices."*

Now I'm sure that this sign was intended with a bit of tongue-in-cheek but no doubt there was a sense of frustration as well. The odd thing is that the sign had been there for many months but the partners hadn't noticed it! It led me to wondering just how much notice the partners in this firm give to their individual staff. The above sign is an indictment upon this firm and its attitude to staff but no more so than the now very extensive evidence available from research that reveals that when it comes to motivating staff most practitioners start from the assumption that employees are ultimately self-interested, proposing performance incentives such as pay increases, promotions, recognition, food and breaks. Rarely do practitioners suggest imbuing the work with greater meaning and purpose. But there's wealth of evidence that people want to do meaningful work: in surveys over three decades, the vast majority of employees have identified meaningful work as the single most important feature that they seek in a job.

I recommend three ways, as a bare minimum, to motivate your staff:

1. Let your employees see for themselves how their work benefits others. Involve your staff in client interviews. Let them meet your clients and be involved in the recommendations and conversations. This was my practice over many years and I recommended this constantly to professional clients. The reaction was invariably the short term concerns of "But what about the cost of having an additional person in the process; what about the effect on productivity?" In the longer term however, and as trust grows, I found that I could delegate more and more to these people as they learned from me and won the confidence of the client and clients began to make their contact directly with the staff member (in the belief too that they could save on fees!). Eventually I was able to

delegate full interview to capable staff. So much so that I actually became concerned as to just how easy this process proved to be…my own ego came into play and I started to wonder, "How come these clients moved so easily?" Gradually I realised however that they still sought the reassurance that I was in the background still taking a strong interest in their affairs and this was reinforced by my deliberate policy to make at least one phone call per month to each of my top 30 clients with the simple question, "How's business?" It never ceased to amaze me just how much new work was inevitably generated through this simple call.

2. Show appreciation to your people but especially let them see and hear the appreciation direct from clients when a job is well done. When clients are positive in their feedback make sure that this message is communicated strongly around the office. Gratitude from the end users is a powerful reminder of the value of continued quality. I recall in my very early days as a very young accountant the firm I worked with had a very strong policy of attempting to calculate or at least estimate the value obtained for the client through the advice we gave. Mostly this was in the area of tax savings but whatever we could find we attempted to spell out both verbally and in a written summary for the client. The extra time spent in doing this was always worthwhile and invariably the value was many times the cost of the client's fees but I think too that the personal feedback that I received from the clients was a great motivator for me.

3. Encourage empathy. As employees develop a deeper understanding of our client's problems and needs they usually become more committed to helping them. They become more likely to make suggestions. A face-to face connection appears to elicit empathy motivating staff to become more involved. I quite

like the approach of a firm that arranges a regular breakfast meeting with key clients and involves all of the team that has involvement with his or her affairs. A no-cost, open discussion with the client, giving the client ample opportunity to ask questions and communicate directly with the people involved in his or her business. The move to outsourcing into India and other countries concerns me for this very reason. The lack of contact and communication has already led to the problem of managers not knowing adequately what is happening in the client's business and being able to answer simple questions from clients such as, "What do you think of that new backhoe I acquired last year?" If you don't know that the client purchased a new backhoe what do you think the reaction will be?

If you facilitate steady progress in meaningful work for your staff, make that progress obvious to them, and treat them fairly and justly (as you would wish to be treated if you were in their position), they will experience the emotions, motivations, and perceptions necessary for greater performance. Their superior work will contribute to organisational success. And here's the beauty of it: they will love their jobs.

CHAPTER SUMMARY

- Employee commitment is a largely neglected realm of management, especially in professional firms, and within it lays a key to success for our professional practices in this rapidly changing world.

- Highly engaged employees outperform disengaged counterparts by up to 28%. The improvement on your bottom line can be up to 57% greater. And then you have the additional challenges of high staff turnover and costs of recruitment where you have disengaged staff.

- Nearly 25 per cent of Australian employees will change jobs this year. And when you consider staff turnover costs are up to 150 per cent of a person's annual salary it's obvious why staff retention is quickly becoming a burning management priority.

- One principal of a practice with over 30 staff has complained to me that if you stand in the hallway of his offices at 5.00 pm on Friday you could easily be killed in the stampede!

- if we can foster an understanding of the bigger picture such as 'building a cathedral' and involve them in our mission or purpose so that there is a sharing of that purpose then I believe we are well on the way to building a hugely successful professional practice.

- A firm's indifference to staff satisfaction and quality issues will be vividly on public display. In addition to speaking to the receptionist one only has to walk through an office to see whether there is pride in appearance, presentation and office layout. If you are not making the effort to instil pride in your workers the quality of your service will also suffer

- I very much like the Balanced Scorecard approach to accountability and management as well as a positive way to involve staff and secure commitment and I highly recommend the use of this process.

- I quote especially (from Harvard Business Journal), "Through exhaustive analysis of diaries kept by knowledge workers, we discovered the progress principle: of all things that can boost emotions, motivation, and perceptions during a workday, the single most important is making progress in meaningful work".

- There's wealth of evidence that people want to do meaningful work: in surveys over three decades, the vast majority of employees have identified meaningful work as the single most important feature that they seek in a job.

- If you facilitate steady progress in meaningful work for your staff, make that progress obvious to them, and treat them fairly and justly (as you would wish to be treated if you were in their position), they will experience the emotions, motivations, and perceptions necessary for greater performance. Their superior work will contribute to organizational success. And here's the beauty of it: they will love their jobs.

CHAPTER 15
TRAINING

I really do despair that so many professional practitioners give so little attention to this important matter of training their people. There is so much waste and lost opportunity for all involved. I am often involved in speaking at national conferences and in panels of discussion. A question that is more common than I care to remember is:

> "But what if I train them and impart all of the skills and knowledge that I've learned over the years – and they up and leave?"

This is a very real possibility if the matters raised in the previous chapter are ignored. My standard response is:

> "But what happens if you don't train them and they stay?

If practitioners are not interested in training themselves, especially, then they won't be too serious about training others.

Many practitioners also look to keeping costs down in this area in order to improve their profit…but are they really? There are also a great many firms that spend large sums on training in only technical matters – much of which is a total waste. I well remember during a visit to a client firm I made myself a cup of coffee in the staff room and noticed a post-it sticker on the fridge calling for volunteers to attend a one-day workshop being presented by a professional body! Who knows whether attendance was relevant or beneficial to the staff member or the firm? What a dreadful way to run your staff training program?

The first step to addressing this challenge I believe is to carry out a skills audit of your firm. What skills are vital to success—obviously your firm will have skills, if yours is an accounting firm, such as tax, audit, analytical and so on but, regardless of your profession, high on your list should be 'emotional intelligence'. It is difficult to find a business journal or book these days that doesn't mention this. A Google search will bring up over 2.5million hits! It is very widely accepted around the world. Emotional Intelligence (EI), often measured as an Emotional Intelligence Quotient (EQ), describes ability, capacity, skill or a self-perceived ability, to identify, assess, and manage the emotions of one's self, of others, and of groups. It is a relatively new area of psychological research. It is now relied upon extensively in addition to IQ. IQ on its own is a good measure of intelligence and someone who has obtained a degree immediately demonstrates high IQ but there are many people in the world who have high IQ but couldn't manage their way out of brown paper bag! It is not unusual to come across an exceptionally intelligent doctor, scientist, lawyer and, yes, accountants who have absolutely no or little 'people' skills and practical common sense. IQ is generally not taught—you have it or you don't and the experts tell us that it can actually decline a little with age. EI however is something that can constantly be improved and grows through training and experience.

It is an acquired skill. So when you have your list of skills required for the practice EI should be high on your list. Then you conduct individual skills audits and attempt to reconcile what you have with what the firm needs. From there you are in a position to establish tailored training for individuals in your firm—including partners! Workshops, courses, continuing education and conferences can all then be locked in and a budget determined. Generation 'Y' has been educated to focus on career paths—if you have tailored training spelled out clearly then you go a long way to satisfying Gen 'Y' in particular but it is understandable that everyone wants to know how to improve themselves and what training is on offer. What is the reality? I have previously mentioned the 'Young

Guns' meetings—training especially aimed at the up and coming staff for development of leadership skills. The testimonials we received from attendees are really quite amazing—they love it and want more.

So when we did a phone around of firms to try to secure additional attendees for a particular meeting, what do you suppose was the most common reaction? "We're too busy". Now does it surprise us why people are leaving many of our professional practices? One very honest practitioner confessed that it really was the partners' fault that bookings hadn't been made pointing out that they do not have any organized program of tailored training in their practice nor do they have any sort of budget for skills development in an organized way. They simply send their people, mostly to technical type conferences, as the mood strikes them in the vain hope that over time individuals will develop the right skills for the firm and feel that they are gaining some training that will help their career.

Anecdotal evidence and experience suggests to me that the vast majority of firms handle their training in this way. Over the years I have seen many of the larger firms establish training budgets in the order of 4-6% of revenue. In this day and age I suspect that this is way too low but even if we suggested 4% for a practice turning over say $3 mill that amounts to $120,000. Many firms would struggle with this sort of 'investment' and we're talking direct costs here only—not time cost. Recruitment is also a major part of the equation in bringing more people into the profession yet time after time advertisements for accounting staff appear in the press that are totally boring! Websites all look the same. Most firms haven't yet realized that the most important reason for a website today is to attract staff—instead we see the same old lists of services, very similar presentations, perhaps a photo of the partners and staff standing in front of the reception with the large firm sign clearly seen overhead and even worse— individual photos of partners in the their best business outfit with their CV's . Gen 'Y' clicks on the hyperlink from say www.seek.com.au and similar sites, takes one look at the firm's website and clicks off never to return. More than ever now you have to sell to your strengths—in a country or suburban practice for example you would now highlight the lower cost of housing, lower fuel costs through less travel, more time with family, no traffic jams, 'green' environment, firm connections as part of larger networks, and so on. Wherever you are based there are good reasons to be there—promote these. A very good training program is something that prospective staff will want to know about and it no longer suffices to simply brush aside this questioning with a simple response, 'Yes we have a lot of training here". They will want to know specifics.

A Whole New Outlook

Ad Hoc decisions in relation to staff recruitment, staff retention and staff training is no longer sufficient. Specific action plans must be thought through carefully and implemented. This requires resources—mostly your time—and unfortunately "we're too busy" simply highlights just how serious your situation really is and the vicious cycle you have entered. Many firms now engage their own professional Human Resources managers—some part-time—and just like the accounting profession their work can be divided into compliance and strategic. If their time is fully absorbed in OH & S issues and other compliance issues only, you have wasted the professional skills of a good HR person. If you have a good HR person, accounting firms in particular have the opportunity also to grow a new revenue stream in looking after the requirements of your business clients as well. UK reports indicate that this is the fastest growing new revenue stream for accounting firms. I haven't come across any Australian firms that have really taken this on seriously although I can think of one that engages a professional HR person on a part time business and the difference that this has made to the practice over time has been nothing short of amazing. Practitioners have no choice but to develop a whole new paradigm—a different way of thinking. If we continue to simply react rather than having well thought out strategies and detailed action plans the flow of staff away from our professions could well become a tidal wave (away from us) because the demand for skilled people in every other facet of business in Australia and New Zealand is now so great that the competitive offerings will soon leave us out of the equation. Already I am aware of at least one university that has around 1200 accounting graduates every year and the majority by far go into the corporate world, government and so on—few if any enter the public practice world.

A White paper produced by IBM in 2008 and titled "The Value of Training" is well worth reading and I quote the following extracts from that paper:

> "Many corporate leaders underestimate the high cost of not training. This paper will provide organisations with an understanding of the costs (and cost areas) a poorly implemented skills development program imposes on an organization as well as the benefits training and skills development can provide. IBM has created recommendations to develop a skills development program using cost effective methods for each employee category in your organization.
>
> THE HIGH COST OF DOING NOTHING
>
> "Untrained or poorly trained users will cost significantly more to support than well-trained workers. Untrained travelling workers who spend a significant portion of their time away from the office,

and who often have networking questions from multiple remote locations, are generally more expensive to support, regardless of the types of devices they're using."

Cost categories may include:

- *Increased down time*
- *Co-worker distraction*
- *Rework*
- *IT/help desk support*

Training also affects employee retention. According to the American Society for Training & Development, 41% of employees at companies with inadequate training programs plan to leave within a year versus 12% of employees at companies who provide excellent training and professional development programs. The cost of replacing skilled employees ranges from US $75,000 to $450,000. The average cost to recruit a professional candidate is $18,374.4 Knowledge and skills development are vital to the health of an organization.

According to a Merrill Lynch study, Motorola estimated that every dollar spent on training yielded US $30 in productivity gains within three years.

Let me highlight that last part in my words… **every $1 spent in training yields $30 in productivity gains in three years!** Surely then the following quote should be placed at the very top of every submission or agenda for discussion on training in a professional practice -

"There is no saturation point in education."

– IBM Founder Thomas J. Watson, Sr.

Start Action Now

Whilst there is a wealth of assistance available on the internet, through books and software you do not have to begin in a complex time consuming manner. I recommend that an initial assessment be carried out for the firm overall to especially identify any shortfalls of deficiencies in your firm particularly with your overall strategic plan in mind. Then proceed to carry out the assessment for each individual with the firm's overall shortfalls very much in mind as you attempt to persuade individuals to build their skills in the shortfall areas. With the information arising from these assessments you are then in a position to prepare a tailored training program for each person and a very detailed budget for training. Accountability for completion can then rest with the individual and when appraisals/ salary reviews are carried out you are in a better position to request the staff member to account for completion of undertakings made for training and to provide evidence of improved skills and value to the firm.

My experience has been that many of the skill shortfalls are usually in the area of 'soft' skills or Emotional Intelligence, i.e., leadership, communication, report writing, negotiation with difficult people, presentation, public speaking, selling skills, and so on. There is a need for strong emphasis in technical skills in professional firms but all too often these soft skills are completely overlooked.

A key piece of information every practice needs to know is what skills and knowledge the practice has. This information is essential for a number of reasons:

- It determines whether the practice can meet the goals set out in its Strategic Plan…assuming it has one!
- Without this information the practice doesn't know where to

improve.

- Training and development is better targeted.

- Recruiting needs are better defined and more likely to result in the most appropriate candidate.

The skills audit is a process that can be used to identify the skill gaps in an organization. The outcome is a training needs analysis that identifies where training is needed.

So a skills audit results in:

- An understanding of the skills required and the gaps the organisation currently has.

- A targeted analysis of development needs.

- A listing of people who need development.

- Data that can be used for purposes such as internal selection.

- Information that can be used for dynamic succession planning.

In the entertainment industry I'm told that success is all about getting 'bums on seats'. Well early in my career I recall the managing partner of the major accounting firm where I worked saying exactly the same thing …but in relation to staff in a professional office. Instead of thinking, "The more staff I have, the more it's costing me" the thinking needs to change to, "The more staff I have, the more revenue we can generate" with the proviso that you are recruiting and training appropriately. Somehow we need to get out of the thinking that people are a cost – people are an investment and as we saw in the chapter on commitment they do want to have purpose and value. As an accountant of course I know that we write off annual salaries in the P & L to determine profit…but just maybe we should re-think this. Really our people are an asset … for the Balance Sheet! If IBM and Motorola insist that every $1 of training returns $30 of extra revenue over three years surely this is one of if not the best investment opportunity you will ever have?

There are so many ways we can look at this to change our paradigm – consider for example a partner /principal charging, for arguments sake $350 per hour. He or she has a personal assistant that costs say $40 per hour. Think of the savings that can be achieved through delegating all administration and general tasks to this personal assistant and then focusing on producing $350 an hour for every hour of additional productivity! The same principle applies through all levels of staffing. Every professional has tasks that can be delegated but once again the proviso is to be sure that they have all the training and resources that are required. Delegate; don't abdicate!

As the business world is continuously changing, organisations will need to provide their employees with training throughout their careers. If they choose not to provide continuous training they will find it difficult to stay ahead of the competition. No matter what the profession, or the size of your practice, training can have a positive effect on performance and a measurable impact on your bottom line.

CHAPTER SUMMARY

• IQ is generally not taught—you have it or you don't and the experts tell us that it can actually decline a little with age. EI however is something that can constantly be improved and grows through training and experience. It is an acquired skill. So when you have your list of skills required for the practice EI should be high on your list. Then you conduct individual skills audits and attempt to reconcile what you have with what the firm needs.

• Most firms haven't yet realized that the most important reason for a website today is to attract staff—instead we see the same old lists of services, very similar presentations, perhaps a photo of the partners and staff standing in front of the reception with the large firm sign clearly seen overhead and even worse— individual photos of partners in the their best business outfit with their CV's . Gen 'Y' clicks on the hyperlink from say www.seek.com.au and similar sites, takes one look at the firm's website and clicks off never to return.

• If we continue to simply react rather than having well thought out strategies and detailed action plans the flow of staff away from our professions could well become a tidal wave (away from us) because the demand for skilled people in every other facet of business in Australia and New Zealand is now so great that the competitive offerings will soon leave us out of the equation.

• Let me highlight in my words... **every $1 spent in training yields $30 in productivity gains in three years!** Surely then the following quote should be placed at the very top of every submission or agenda for discussion on training in a professional practice –

> *"There is no saturation point in education."*
> *– IBM Founder Thomas J. Watson, Sr.*

- My experience has been that many of the skill shortfalls are usually in the area of 'soft' skills or Emotional Intelligence, i.e., leadership, communication, report writing, negotiation with difficult people, presentation, public speaking, selling skills, and so on. There is a need for strong emphasis in technical skills in professional firms but all too often these soft skills are completely overlooked.

- In the entertainment industry I'm told that success is all about getting 'bums on seats'. Well early in my career I recall the managing partner of the major accounting firm where I worked saying exactly the same thing …but in relation to staff in a professional office. Instead of thinking, "The more staff I have, the more it's costing me" the thinking needs to change to, "The more staff I have, the more revenue we can generate" with the proviso that you are recruiting and training appropriately. Somehow we need to get out of the thinking that people are a cost – people are an investment and as we saw in the chapter on commitment they do want to have purpose and value.

- As the business world is continuously changing, organizations will need to provide their employees with training throughout their careers. If they choose not to provide continuous training they will find it difficult to stay ahead of the competition. No matter what the profession, or the size of your practice, training can have a positive effect on performance and a measurable impact on your bottom line.

CHAPTER 16
PARTNER COMPENSATION

Or getting your fair share of the carrot!

Compensation of partners in professional firms has always been contentious. Of late, however, there has been a noticeable attempt by firms to take the best from previous systems and try to blend this with new developments in firm management.

Most firms have remained with the 'equal' approach however many are now suggesting that whilst easy it promotes mediocrity as the firm becomes larger. There is a range of methods from this 'equal' approach to the 'Balanced Scorecard' approach which is very new to the professionals and has been referred to in previous chapters. I am an advocate of this latter approach but know of very few professional firms at present utilizing it and I am very keen to assist firms to do so and more especially to hear from firms that have successfully (or otherwise) implemented this process.

Unfortunately most of our present, rather comfortable, measuring is based upon lagging indicators rather than leading indicators. The following comments are based upon notes I made with the intention of encouraging discussion and debate with feedback to me. I would love to hear from readers as to your views on this issue dear to the hearts of us all.

Underlying Assumptions

• The way in which any individual is compensated is likely to affect his/her actions. Partners in professional firms are no exception.

To the extent though that the way in which compensation is determined is not aligned with a firm's strategic goals it is unlikely that those firm goals will be achieved.

• If there is a change in the competitive environment in which a firm is operating there is likely to be a need for the firm to change its competitive strategy.

• If a change in firm strategy is deemed necessary to respond to changing environmental factors then it is highly probable that this will necessarily call for a change in the way partner compensation is determined.

• All professions are undergoing change today that can best be described as akin to a Tsunami. Corporate consolidations continue at a strong pace. There is a war for talent in securing quality staff. Computer software and hardware continue to improve at an ever-increasing, compounding rate. New communications media leave many of the older generations completely confounded. Outsourcing to India and other countries is seen as increasingly acceptable. Ethics and good business practices are increasingly under stress. Many professional practitioners are feeling the effects of stress and depression. Life Balance is the goal of every professional. And the list continues..... It is not all negative of course. Incomes in most professions are now higher than ever and change creates opportunity.

Some issues concerning compensation and their strategic implications:

• Short v. Long Term - how to deal with the need for immediate payoff v. investment in the future of the firm. Professional firm partners tend to seek drawings in favour of investing in the long-term value of the firm. This is especially so when older partners are close to retirement.

• Technicians, Managers and Entrepreneurs v. respective value contributions. Each has much value to offer a professional firm but how does a firm account for this?

• Management by committee/ management structure. Partnerships are effectively 'management by committee' and invariably the question is unanswered as to who is first amongst equals? Who is the leader?

• Locus of Interest (individual v. the Firm). Conflicts of interest abound.

• How is partner equity created and realized (valuation of goodwill)?

Surprisingly some firms ignore Goodwill for ease of introducing new partners and succession but realistically Goodwill doesn't go away. All that is happening is that it is quietly growing in the background for the benefit of future partners when the practice is eventually sold, listed, etc.

• Risk aversion/ security/ power/ control issues.

• Founder values.

• Impact of firm size.

• Differences in lifestyle preferences. This has been apparent in virtually every practice I have seen.

• How do you calculate partner salaries?

• Why people seek partner status?

• Career aspiration.

• Increased compensation.

• Managerial responsibility.

• Need for control.

• Need to create career and financial security.

• Why are people invited to become partner?

• Promise on appointment.

• Retain/ acquire technical skill.

- Contact network.
- Firm merger.
- Succession considerations.
- Work responsibility e.g. in the accounting profession - sign off audits, tax returns, etc.
- Components of Compensation.
- Goodwill.
- Salary.
- Return on Equity.
- Super Profits.
- Partner Salary Calculations. There are obviously many ways to calculate partner salaries and in the case of at least one 'Big 4' firm today my observation is that almost everyone is described as a 'partner' from manager, up!.

However there are at least four basic measures:

° Market – what would that partner realistically generate as a salary in the open market?

° Rule of thumb – what are the large institutions using as a benchmark   – the figure varies considerably but anecdotal feedback indicates an incredibly wide range in Australia. Figures in the order of $120,000 to $150,000 are apparent in some of the smaller firms.

° Take the salary and charge rate of the highest paid staff member, e.g, say $60,000 and $150/hr. Then look at the partner charge rate, say $200/hr. What we are saying in these circumstances is that through charge rates we have assessed that partners have a premium of 33⅓% over the staff member therefore applying that same premium to partner salaries we would arrive at a salary of $80,000.

° Most firms apply a multiple to professional staff salaries to arrive at the individual charge rate, i.e., 3 times, 4 times, etc. and therefore the fees turnover expected from that staff member as an individual. Use that same multiplier in reverse on partner generated fees, e.g. say $200,000 fees generated by the individual partner – divide that by the multiple, say, 3, in this instance salary would be $66,667.

- **Some Criteria for evaluating Partner Performance.**
- New client growth.
- Net fee realisation growth.
- New services to existing & new clients.
- Higher hourly realization.
- Realizable hours and average $ recovery attributable to the Partner.
- Demonstrable improvement in technical competency.
- Improvement in quality of team members' skill set and productivity.
- Other contributions to the firm's professional capability.
- Client attrition.
- Feedback from Team Members.
- True profitability and how can it be assessed

Obviously this list, although lengthy, is not an exhaustive one but there is much room for discussion and debate.

This is how one firm approached the question of compensation:
Each Partner has his/her own list of clients for whom he/she was responsible. The Partner responsible for the Business Consulting Division does not have a perpetual client list. Where there is an obvious bad fit between client and partner/manager the client is invited to be serviced by another partner or manager. Each Partner also had Portfolio Responsibility for certain aspects of the firm e.g.

• IT

• Quality Assurance, research & Development, Professional Associations and Professional Indemnity.

• Human Resources.

• Supplier Management.

• Marketing.

• Finance.

• General Management—Managing Partner.

At the Annual Partner Retreat each Partner would present his/her planning goals for the following year. This would take the form of a business plan and personal commitment statement that would include:

• A summary of his/her projected realisation by client, service line and team member

• A gross profit contribution projection after allowing for estimated team member compensation and standard hourly variable costs.

• A projected cash flow statement based on WIP turn and receivables collection targets

• A summary of specific (and where possible, measurable) out-comes in relation to his/her Portfolio.

• Other specific projects or initiatives he/she intends (or would like) to pursue during the year.

• The background work for these presentations would in fact have been done between and amongst the partners prior to the Annual Retreat so that there was consistency and realism.

• At the end of the year the partner would be reviewed in relation to his/her objectives and targets although throughout the year at the monthly partners' meeting these issues would be discussed if and when relevant.

• The Partnership Agreement provides for the dismissal of an under performing partner subject to certain safeguards for the individual.

• After the Partner Review the partners would evaluate the firm's overall performance in relation to competitors and its targets for the year. It would revisit its strategic plan and review its SWOTs.

• Having regard to the past year, the strategic plan and an assessment of the current economic climate the partners would set a realistic but challenging profit goal (before any consideration of individual partner compensation) for the next year.

• This would be translated into the required hourly realization after consideration of:

  º Micro review of major clients' expected needs, e.g. one page plans for each major client.

  º Estimated new client growth

  º Estimated client attrition

• Utilizing the partners individually prepared business plans they would project:

  º The number of team members required

  º Hourly time budgets and average hourly realization for each person in the firm

  º Fee revenue would also be projected by Service Line and Partner Client List

This would form the basis for the firm's final annual business plan. I have facilitated numerous Strategic Planning workshops for firms and it is a distinct advantage to complete a workshop prior to finalising the detail the emphasis at the workshop being to clarify strategies and prioritise issues.

Some adjustments will need to be made for rate changes and other things following discussions with team members etc. Over the years I have utilised what I refer to as a 'five-way' budget that in affect allows for 'what if' scenarios where changes can be made with instant calculations throughout the budget to produce final results.

• The question of compensation for the next year is then discussed. The compensation model is:

º A salary component that may not be equal for all partners (but usually is)

º A return based on equity

º The distribution of profit above the sum of the above two components called the Super Profit.

º Salary component: consideration is given to the person's experience, what he/she might reasonably expect to be paid in an employee position, what other things he/she does for or brings to the practice.

º Equity Return : this is where Goodwill is valued and each partner receives his/her share of the return on goodwill based on his/her equity holding.

º In valuing goodwill the firm looks at the previous year's earnings and adjusts for non recurring revenues or expenses. It gets back to what it describes as 'hard core' earnings. It deducts partners' salaries from this figure and capitalizes the residual at an agreed rate - say 30%. For example: suppose hard core earnings are $1.25 million and partners salaries were $500,000 in total. The goodwill at 30% cap rate would be $2.5 million (1.25m - 500k x 1.3).

º The figure for goodwill would be used for the following 12 months in the case of a partner's death, dismissal or retirement from the practice.

º The view is that goodwill attaches to the firm but is owned by the constituents in proportion to their equity. The more senior members are likely to have more equity and so get a higher return but they have been there longer and have contributed more to the firm's reputation and position. They also give up relatively more in comparison with a straight equity split when salaries and super profit are fixed.

° Distribution of Super Profit—if there is an excess of profit over total salaries and return on equity (goodwill) it is distributed equally. If there is a deficiency it is also distributed equally. The view is taken that if all of the partners are not making an equal contribution the offending person should be asked to retire from the partnership.

° By having an equal split of super profit there is a strong incentive for junior partners to work harder for incremental profit above the level at which Return on Equity has been reached - that's why valuing Goodwill too high can have a negative impact on junior partner performance. There is also a strong incentive for junior partners to get more equity.

° Partner Compensation

° The following table shows how it would work when ... $1.5 million total profit before partners' salaries, Goodwill previously valued at $2.5 million 5 partners with different equity shares and one partner receiving a lower salary than the others.

Partner	Equity	Salary	Return on Equity	Super Profit	Total
A	25%	115,000	187,500	38,000	340,500
B	25%	115,000	187,500	38,000	340,500
C	20%	115,000	150,000	38,000	303,000
D	15%	115,000	112,500	38,000	265,500
E	15%	100,000	112,500	38,000	250,500
TOTAL	100%	580,000	750,000	190,000	1,500,000

Note: the senior equity partners give up $35,000 compared with a straight equity split but the view they take is that they would not make $340,500 on their own. If that were not the case they would be financially better off to have their own firm. In other words, they accept that value attaches to the firm as a whole as well as to their personal contribution - a contribution that can only be fully realized because the firm exists.

I have encountered such a variety of partner compensation arrangements I suspect that I could write a book on its own on the subject. I recall a situation when as a very young, new partner (with 5 small children and a big mortgage on my house) in a 300 partner firm, the newly elected Australian Managing partner decided to take a hard line on high Work-in-Progress and Debtor levels and announced that there would be 'no more partner drawings' until the national level of WIP and Debtors was reduced to a level he determined! Six months without cash for 300 partners certainly achieved the desired result – I can't recall though whether he was voted in for a second term.

Another very large firm introduced a policy that as soon as a debtor or WIP balance reached 30 days and 60 days respectively it was transferred as a debit entry to the individual current account of the partner responsible and not brought back until rectified.   A much smaller firm introduced very complex arrangements of interest penalties and bonuses. The exercise of completing the monthly calculations was a nightmare and needless to say created much angst with partners.

There is also a trend for firms to establish an annual bonus pool, often 10% of annual net profit of the firm, for distribution to partners who have performed particularly well in a given year. The 'carrot' can take many forms. Very broadly speaking and based upon my personal experience with many firms we could summarize these as follows:

EQUAL PARTNERS

Simple to work with but leads to mediocrity in larger firms.

FORMULA

The more complex, it seems the better for many firms.

SPREADSHEET

Based upon the pen and paper system only these days automated - accountants in particular love spreadsheets and will always argue a strong case that they have the best model.

MANAGING PARTNER DECISION

Effectively this is a CEO model of managing business – just a different title. Unfortunately though the managing partner is usually heavily involved in client work as well.

COMPENSATION COMMITTEE

Seems to work reasonably well in large firms.

POINTS /UNITS

Used in very large firms. I personally worked under this system for close to 20 years. Politics and lobbying play a major role.

BALANCED SCORECARD

Very new to professional service firms.

The following shows where these are generally used:

System	2-3 Partners	4-7 Partners	8-10 Partners	10+ Partners
Equal	Common	Rare	Never	Never
Formula	Common	Very Common	Less Common	Seldom
Spreadsheet	Rare	Effective at Upper end	More Common	Too difficult
Managing Partner Decision	Rare	Not Uncommon	Too Difficult	More so
Compensation Committee	Not Used	Not Used	Becomes more Common	Common, especially in consolidator models
Points/Units	Not Used	Not Used	Not Used	Not Uncommon
Balanced Scorcard	Will work in any size firm that has a strategic Plan and strong leadership			

Balanced Scorecard

It does seem to me that the area where professionals reveal their most creative skills is in this area of profit share or compensation. There is no limit to the possible options. It is fair to say though that often what works for one firm will not work for another. Whatever model is chosen must work for that particular firm and reflect its values. Sometimes though partners don't get a choice. I have seen too many firms where a senior partner holds a majority interest and takes absolute control ignoring the wishes of junior partners. Inevitably serious problems arise. Most models will contain some element of subjective judgement. The people who make that subjective judgement must have the trust and respect of other people and all too often this is lacking.

CHAPTER SUMMARY

• Most firms have remained with the 'equal' approach however many are now suggesting that whilst easy it promotes mediocrity as the firm becomes larger.

• Unfortunately most of our present, rather comfortable, measuring is based upon lagging indicators rather than leading indicators.

• I have encountered such a variety of partner compensation arrangements I suspect that I could write a book on its own on the subject. I recall a situation when as a very young, new partner (with 5 small children and a big mortgage on my house) in a 300-partner firm, the newly elected Australian Managing partner decided to take a hard line on high Work-in-Progress and Debtor levels and announced that there would be 'no more partner drawings' until the national level of WIP and Debtors was reduced to a level he determined! Six months without cash for 300 partners certainly achieved the desired result.

• It does seem to me that the area where professionals reveal their most creative skills is in this area of profit share or compensation. There is no limit to the possible options.

CHAPTER 17
THE PRACTICE OF THE FUTURE

Some Crystal Ball Gazing

As I move from firm to firm, network meeting to network meeting, I have the opportunity to focus on what the practice of the future might look like. The more innovative firms are already moving rapidly in new directions whilst the vast majority, the 'late adopters' and 'laggards' wonder what is happening. It is probably fair to say that the majority of firms that I work with are the 'innovative' and 'early adopter' firms by the very fact that they are seeking solutions, ideas and directions.

As a general statement there is an overall trend to recognizing that a firm is a business and requires management.

The first step is to recognize the need for change. You cannot change what you do not acknowledge and what you do not acknowledge is going to get worse until you do.

Practitioners are very reluctant to admit that they might be average or below. People fear change. As a result they respond by refusing to work together, blaming each other for problems and generating disinformation. To overcome this, we need to be aware of these responses and be able to support people through their concerns. Refer to my earlier comments in this book relating to Locus of Control. Complacency is real. The first step is to be honest about what needs fixing—it's a bit like alcoholics anonymous—you can't fix what you don't acknowledge. Regardless of the size of your firm, to successfully manage change there are some key requirements and these include:

- Open and honest communications;
- Establishment of trust and respect;
- Mutual understanding;
- Accurate information about strengths and weaknesses;
- A willingness to learn and a culture that supports it; and
- Development of new skills and ways of working.

Why do we need to Change?

Let's consider just some of the reasons, many of which have already been canvassed in this book but in summary:

- Productivity levels in many of our professions are invariably very low. I usually find that there is at least 20% unrecorded or unaccounted for time, i.e., free time given to clients. There is enormous untapped value in tightening up, training, and carrying out waste audits for professional firms.

- In an era of Continuous Improvement processes, TQM, Corporate Re-engineering, Sixth Sigma, Strategic Planning, Strategic SWOTS, Pareto Analysis, Forcefield Analysis, Mind Mapping, Balanced Scorecard, a revolution in communication media, social networking, cloud computing, and much, much more - absolute revolutions in the business world, we professionals often wallow in our complacency and are the last bastion of resistance to change! Most practitioners would not know what these processes are about! Only a minority of firms have a Strategic Planning Process. Some have "Lists" of issues but no real prioritisation, action plans or coordination with an overall vision and values for the practice.

- Many principals do not understand requirements of and the need for training our people in generic or soft skills nor the fact that young professionals are seeking a stronger emphasis on life balance and shorter term goals. Recruiting and retaining them requires specific action plans that work.

• Although the 'Baby Boomer' succession issues are strongly documented in the media and press few firms have addressed this issue seriously or have a formal plan in place.

• Many firms continue as compliance sweat shops in 'compliance lock', despite ongoing comprehensive surveys and reports, including for the accounting profession over 15 years ago, a report by the ANZ Bank calling for additional value-added support to small and medium size enterprises (SME's)

• The 'India' solution is gaining momentum with many firms now seeking recruitment of experienced professionals in India, Malaysia and other low salary cost countries.

• The image of some professions including especially my own remains unattractive to the young (for no valid reason).

• Time management skills—there is little or no training in building these skills.

• HR (Human Resources) is the fastest growing new service for accountants in the UK—yet in Australia many practitioners often ask me "What is HR?"

• The move to corporatisation is fast moving with many acquisitions, mergers and consolidations quietly taking place in Australia and New Zealand, whilst in America this appears to have developed into frenzy.

• Clients are lifting their expectations.

• Females in number now dominate many professions and have different priorities and needs to males (I am not being sexist here – simply stating a significant change).

• The partnership structure is now out-dated—who is the first amongst equals—is anyone truly leading?

• Globalisation cannot be ignored—consider a computer virus in, say, China; can knock out whole enterprises elsewhere in the world within 24 hours or less.

• Increased capital requirements to buy in and to invest in firms means less professionals will have the resources to buy into partnerships.

• With increasing leverage fewer principals or partners may be required.

• The accelerating IT development, change and transition generally.

• Net Profit - if most firms calculated correctly to provide for proper commercial salaries and ROI (including Goodwill) Net profit would range from only 5-10%.

Once again, this listing is by no means a comprehensive list and I would be very confident that readers could create equally lengthy additional lists.

It's Your Choice!

No one can order change—it must be persuaded but we have to decide that change is needed and take the first step, Many practitioners will continue to spin on their wheels in the belief that they 'cannot afford' the time or resources to do so and will pay the penalty in the long term.

Some Trends & Strategies for the Practice of the Future

The following are just some trends and strategies that I have seen implemented in recent years:

• Regular practice 'waste' audits.

• Regular practice and individual skills audits.

• Tailoured training.

• Full implementation and training in value pricing and fixed price agreements for clients.

• Development of new services with an emphasis on client needs, e.g. using One-Page Plans for each 'A' Client.

• Full and proper categorization of all clients.

• Screening of clients, culling of clients and exit interviews of clients.

• Implementation of intranet systems, job monitoring, full utilization of websites, cloud computing, the new communications media and social networking.

• A regular strategic planning process involving continuous improvement with prioritized action plans and specific project teams.

• Increased training in generic skills with overall training in the order of 5-6% or more of revenue.

• Stronger leverage in equity participation, greater staff leverage, much stronger leverage of computer hardware and software, greater knowledge leverage and, through all of these, greater leverage of value. Already we have clients (professional service firms) with staff leverage of 30-40 people to one partner. The leverage you choose (remember the choice is yours!) will depend upon the vision for your practice arising from your strategic planning process.

• Net Profit calculated on corporate lines, i.e. after allowing for commercial salaries for 'principals' and realistic ROI will be more in the order of 20-25%.

• Professional firms will have greater demand for investment and this will increase the value of practices.

• Practices will be managed professionally by 'CEO's'/Practice Managers who have detailed role descriptions and full authority for operational decisions.

• Full HR systems and processes that focus on strategy will be implemented with this service also provided to clients in the case of accounting professionals.

• The focus of services much more upon adding value in meeting clients' specific needs in a range of areas and where the firm itself does not have the skills needed, very strong alliances have been developed with other firms or organizations to provide that support.

• A stronger trend to Fixed Income 'partners', i.e. no equity and varying layers of equity participation.

• A formal and regular process of 'partner'/principal appraisals that review performance and help these people individually.

• Globalised standards.

• Consumer power…only recently I read of a consumer organisation that is forming groups of home owners with mortgages to negotiate as one with banks on interest rates, fees and other charges. The first group , I understand has 1,000 home owners!

• Momentum is king.

• 'iConnectedness' for communications.

Again, this is by no means a comprehensive list, but it does represent a glimpse at the practice of the future and if you believe any of these to be fanciful—think again! I have clients now doing some or all of these things. Each of these strategies is in use now—somewhere. They are achievable, but without a specific Business Plan, the odds are stacked against you. All too often we are too busy fighting the crocodiles to consider an overall strategy such as draining the swamp! Can you also afford to remain complacent about your own business?

CHAPTER SUMMARY

• As a general statement there is an overall trend to recognizing that a firm is a business and requires management. The first step is to recognize the need for change. You cannot change what you do not acknowledge and what you do not acknowledge is going to get worse until you do.

• Clients are lifting their expectations.

• Many practitioners will continue to spin on their wheels in the belief that they 'cannot afford' the time or resources to do so and will pay the penalty in the long term.

• Without a specific Business Plan, the odds are stacked against you. All too often we are too busy fighting the crocodiles to consider an overall strategy such as draining the swamp! Can you also afford to remain complacent about your own business?

CHAPTER 18
.......IN SUMMARY

MANY PRACTITIONERS ARE AS HAPPY AS A PIG IN MUD!

As I travel around Australia and New Zealand (110 trips just in the last two years!) and meet hundreds of accounting practitioners—virtually on a daily basis—I become increasingly convinced that the majority of practitioners probably are actually quite happy with their lot and although they often recognize that change is inevitable these particular practitioners have no great motivation for change. More and more I find myself working with the firms that are keen to move forward—the innovative firms that want to change and that are looking for new ideas and ways of improving their firms but these are in the minority overall.

The rest, the majority, appear as happy as , excuse the analogy, a pig in mud—complacent to the goings on in the world and happy to receive 'slops' on a daily basis! They are busy, busy, busy—doing it, doing it, doing it—scratching around in the mud without realizing that there is a better world. Quite happy to sunbake in the sun they have become very complacent and satisfied with their lot. Many take the view "We're accountants, why would we need help? We can look after ourselves" (and most other professionals share that attitude). The official ABS statistics reveal quite a different story—in fact they show that accountancy practitioners , in the main, are actually very poor business managers—working very long hours for below average returns.

For these particular practitioners I believe it is a case of you cannot change what you do not acknowledge. And what you do not acknowledge is going to get worse until you do.

Firms are usually very reluctant to admit that they just might be average or below.

One measure that I use and it is only one measure is the Practice Recovery rate—NOT Practice Charge rate often used by firms—but the total staff and partners recovery rate across the entire practice. It's a bit like Alcoholics Anonymous—until you recognize you have a problem there is little you can do to fix it—join Accountants Anonymous today! The first step is to be honest about what needs fixing. Once you have acknowledged the existence of a problem and your ownership of it, living with the status quo becomes much more difficult.

I have long believed that the solution to any problem lies in correctly defining the problem – unfortunately many practitioners cannot see the problem. Accountancy practitioners in particular have also been described as the last bastion of resistance to change! We are a very, very careful lot and like to examine every situation to minimize risk—it's part of our training– but unfortunately all too often we go too far and become entangled in paralysis from analysis.

Some time ago Harvard Business Review published an excellent article on leadership qualities and types. One is described as the 'Expert' leader and accountants are mentioned as being dominant in this type of leadership. One of the qualities of this leader is the 'expert' approach..... I'm the expert here and it is 'my way or the highway'. As a result when a partners' meeting is held chances are we will find a room full of 'expert' leaders—all believing that their own point of view is the correct one. The question of who is 'first amongst equals' is not easily resolved and individuals with a particular barrow to push can become dominant on particular issues.

For this same reason Strategic Planning sessions and Business Plans will often be hijacked by the dominant personalities with particular issues to pursue. Often strategies for a firm that reflect what is happening in the wider market place and have higher value to the firm are completely missed. The thinking can become very inward focused to the point where external factors are barely addressed—or for that matter known! Very, very few firms have a suitable process for strategic planning and pulling together a dynamic business plan. Many will insist they do but when I examine these invariably I find what amounts to no more than a list or agenda of issues to be dealt with—mostly operational issues rather than strategic. There is usually little attempt to prioritise action plans arising from these issues and firms often have far too much to take on after a strategic meeting with the result that little or nothing gets implemented. And they wonder why!

I have also found firms that have used external facilitators but often these external facilitators lack direct experience and knowledge of the professional service firm so once again the strategies settled upon within the meeting are restricted to the experience of the partners.
It is easy to move headlong into a strategy without knowing about the pitfalls—for example many firms in the accounting profession have commenced implementing fixed pricing agreements and quite a few have experienced substantial write-offs in the first year. The reason is that the timesheet system that they have relied upon for many years was not being used correctly with staff and partners not recording or 'hiding' time (usually 20% plus in an average firm) and they become more relaxed with the fixed pricing system—now comfortable about recording time and that 20% plus suddenly turns up! It is important to ensure that the timesheet system is being used correctly before relying on previous renderings as a basis for the new fixed price.

One of the first questions a practitioner needs to ask is "How much do I need to earn?" and I have discovered that this figure varies significantly from practitioner to practitioner and from firm to firm but if there are practitioners earning say $500,000 to over $1,500,000 net profit (and I have clients in this range who are working smarter not harder) why do so many practitioners settle for less than $100,000? The lowest I have seen is $30,000 and my advice to that practitioner was to work for someone else!

The Institute of Chartered Accountants in England & Wales have produced an outstanding report titled "the Profitable and Sustainable Practice" (contact me for details) wherein they have identified two distinct types of practice—what they call the 'Lifestyle' practice and the 'Enterprising' practice. In my view there is a third which is a mixture of these two. There can be no doubt that some practitioners are seeking 'lifestyle' in preference to 'enterprising' (or corporate) practice. Why not enjoy both?

Working smarter is about identifying niche markets and clients and leveraging up with systems, pricing and skilled staff. It can be done! David Maister (international professional services guru, author & speaker) is an obvious example of someone who has leveraged on price or value. He is a sole operator who I understand earns an income that most professionals would only dream of. On the other hand there are now many sole practitioners who have leveraged staff to 30 and more per partner, utilizing very tight systems and procedures and I suspect in the very near future this will become the norm.

For those who want to build a business of value, rather than a stream of personal income dependent upon hours and hard work, a shift in thought processes needs to take place this is unlikely to come from within the firm—external stimulus is usually required.

The work/life balance is also a crucial factor—and not just for partners/principals. Brighter graduates are much more cynical, they understand job insecurities better, and they don't trust their employers to put their staff before profitability. Some large firms and especially large corporations have done a great deal of damage here. Loyalty to a firm tends to be much more short term now. As a result there is greater focus on HR issues and developing an appropriate 'culture' for your firm. But most practices are clearly not taking these messages to heart. Alternatively they may believe that the necessary changes can be dealt with on traditional timescales; only time will tell whether that is right but my assessment is that time is running out!

Are you as happy as a 'pig in mud' or would you prefer to soar with the eagles?

...and Finally...

What are the main features of a successful professional services firm? Regardless of size, sector and location the features that they have in common include that they:

- Have written dynamic business plans and mission statements;
- Ensure that their people work cooperatively and flexibly;
- Set high targets and benchmark themselves against other organisations (not necessarily their own profession);
- Use financial performance as a measure of success rather than a driver;
- Have and continue to achieve improvements as a measure of success rather than a driver;

•Have processes of continuous improvement in internal efficiency through the integration of technology and comprehensive processes and systems in the way that they work;

• Invest and continue to invest in technology;

• Invest and continue to invest in training, especially the soft or generic skills training;

• Have a clear client focus and have changed the way they work and how they respond to their client's needs;

• Meet with their clients regularly to check their perception of service delivery and establish their clients specific needs;

•Have established clearly their sustainable competitive advantage and continue to build their reputation in their unique services;

• Have good self-knowledge;

• Have good competitor knowledge;

• Have good client knowledge;

• Have good technical knowledge;

• Have good staff knowledge;

• Do not become distracted chasing every opportunity through trying to be all things to all people;

• Have established strong alliances with other organisations and networks and are happy to share their experiences as well as learn from others;

• Continue to audit their skill base and adjust their structure to cope with change as it arises;

• Strongly utilise facilitators with direct experience in their own field to assist in management of change; and

• Attract and retain high-quality professionals.

Professional practitioners and their firms have the opportunity of a powerful future and many are grasping the opportunities. Current trends indicate that knowledge will become highly valuable and professionals have the ability to be key players rather than last bastions of resistance to change. As the pace of change accelerates (as it is!) and the complexity of life increases professionals will be able to use their intellect to develop innovative solutions. You can create our own success. I trust that my thoughts and experience expressed in this book encourage you to pick up the baton and run or start a conversation you haven't had or haven't concluded. Just do it! From time to time an attendee at a conference will come up to me and say something like, "I've heard it all before". My upbringing has taught me to be polite but I have been very tempted to say, "Yes, but have you done anything about it…if you had you wouldn't be here!" Once again, **"Just do it."**

CHAPTER SUMMARY

• The rest, the majority, appear as happy as , excuse the analogy, a pig in mud—complacent to the goings on in the world and happy to receive 'slops' on a daily basis! They are busy, busy, busy—doing it, doing it, doing it—scratching around in the mud without realizing that there is a better world. Quite happy to sunbake in the sun they have become very complacent and satisfied with their lot.

• I have long believed that the solution to any problem lies in correctly defining the problem – unfortunately many practitioners cannot see the problem. Accountancy practitioners in particular have also been described as the last bastion of resistance to change! We are a very, very careful lot and like to examine every situation to minimize risk—it's part of our training– but unfortunately all too often we go too far and become entangled in paralysis from analysis.

• Strategic Planning sessions and Business Plans will often be hijacked by the dominant personalities with particular issues to pursue. Often strategies for a firm that reflect what is happening in the wider market place and have higher value to the firm are completely missed. The thinking can become very inward focused to the point where external factors are barely addressed—or for that matter known!

• One of the first questions a practitioner needs to ask is "How much do I need to earn?" and I have discovered that this figure varies significantly from practitioner to practitioner and from firm to firm but if there are practitioners earning say $500,000 to over $1,500,000 net profit (and I have clients in this range who are working smarter not harder) why do so many practitioners settle for less than $100,000? The lowest I have seen is $30,000 and my advice to that practitioner was to work for someone else!

- Professional practitioners and their firms have the opportunity of a powerful future and many are grasping the opportunities. Current trends indicate that knowledge will become highly valuable and professionals have the ability to be key players rather than last bastions of resistance to change.

- You can create our own success. I trust that my thoughts and experience expressed in this book encourage you to pick up the baton and run or start a conversation you haven't had or haven't concluded. Just do it!

To contact the author

P: +61 2 6922 6565

F: +61 2 69 22 5351

PO Box 88, Wagga Wagga NSW 2650

ABN: 26 717 685 360

Web: www.businessventurers.com.au

E: david@businessventurers.com.au

INDEX